SURVIVAL GUIDE
FOR INTERNS

BLACKWELL'S
SURVIVAL GUIDE FOR INTERNS

Mustafa Hammad

Assistant Clinical Instructor
Internal Medicine and Neurology Residency
University Hospital and Medical Center
State University of New York at Stony Brook

b

**Blackwell
Science**

©2002 by Mustafa Hammad

Blackwell Science, Inc.
Editorial Offices:
  Commerce Place, 350 Main Street, Malden, Massachusetts 02148, USA
  Osney Mead, Oxford OX2 OEL, England
  25 John Street, London WC1N 2BS, England
  23 Ainslie Place, Edinburgh EH3 6AJ, Scotland
  54 University Street, Carlton, Victoria 3053, Australia

Other Editorial Offices:
  Blackwell Wissenschafts-Verlag GmbH, Kurfürstendamm 57, 10707 Berlin,
    Germany
  Blackwell Science KK, MG Kodenmacho Building, 7-10 Kodenmacho
    Nihombashi, Chuo-ku, Tokyo 104, Japan
  Iowa State University Press, A Blackwell Science Company, 2121 S. State
    Avenue, Ames, Iowa 50014-8300, USA

Distributors:

The Americas
  Blackwell Publishing
  c/o AIDC
  P.O. Box 20
  50 Winter Sport Lane
  Williston, VT 05495-0020
  (Telephone orders: 800-216-
    2522; fax orders: 802-864-
    7626)

Australia
  Blackwell Science Pty, Ltd.
  54 University Street
  Carlton, Victoria 3053
  (Telephone orders: 03-9347-
    0300;
  fax orders: 03-9349-3016)

Outside the Americas and Australia
  Blackwell Science, Ltd.
  c/o Marston Book Services, Ltd.
  P.O. Box 269
  Abingdon
  Oxon OX14 4YN
  England
  (Telephone orders: 44-01235-
    465500;
  fax orders: 44-01235-465555)

Acquisitions: Beverly Copland
Development: Amy Nuttbrock
Production: Shawn Girsberger
Manufacturing: Lisa Flanagan
Marketing Manager: Toni Fournier

Cover design by Gary Ragaglia
Typeset by Modern Graphics, Inc.
Printed and bound by Sheridan Books
  Inc.

Printed in the United States of America
01 02 03 04 5 4 3 2 1

The Blackwell Science logo is a trade mark of Blackwell Science Ltd.,
registered at the United Kingdom Trade Marks Registry

Library of Congress Cataloging-in-Publication Data

Hammad, Mustafa.
  Blackwell's medical intern survival guide / author, Mustafa Hammad.
    p. ; cm.
  ISBN 0-632-04589-2 (pbk.)
  1. Interns (Medicine)—Handbooks, manuals, etc.
  [DNLM: 1. Internship and Residency.   WX 203 H224b 2002]   I. Title:
Medical intern survival guide.   II. Title.
  RA972 .H26 2002
  610'.71'55—dc21

                              2001003441

To mom and dad for their guidance and support throughout the years, thank you.

Contents

Contents

Foreword

Medical school provides a foundation in the basic and clinical sciences. While we are students, we have the opportunity to develop and apply these clinical skills during the third year clerkship and fourth year subinternship. At graduation, we feel a sense of accomplishment but also unease about the upcoming challenges of internship. For many, internship and residency are the most demanding experiences of our careers. New hospitals, an unrelenting workload, increased responsibilities, and a spectrum of personalities to negotiate undermine the hard won confidence of the graduating student. *Blackwell's Survival Guide for Interns* is an invaluable tool to help you prepare and succeed as an intern.

The knowledge and the skills we develop as medical students are limited when compared to the multitude of challenges that face the intern. The first chapter of *Blackwell's Survival Guide for Interns* (Chapter 1: "The Internship Synopsis") provides invaluable information an intern needs to succeed in the hospital environment: how to develop a productive relationship with nurses, fellow house officers, and other members of the health care team; presenting and charting of patients; the importance of your relationship with the patients and their families. Basic survival skills (organization, eating, and sleeping) are also covered. This chapter should be read before starting on the wards.

We all want to be good interns but what constitutes a good intern is dependent on one's perspective. The results of two surveys of students, interns, residents, attending physicians, nurses, and (importantly) patients on what constitutes a good intern are presented and analyzed in Chapter 2. These data, collected from several hospitals and with the analyses by Dr. Hammad, provide interns with a unique understanding of how they are viewed by others, and how they can be successful and caring physicians. The survey results and insightful analyses will make useful reading throughout one's career.

Evidenced-based medicine (EBM) has become an important method of effectively using the medical literature to provide the best care for our patients and to educate ourselves. In Chapter 3, Dr. Hammad has succinctly outlined the techniques of EBM and, by using practical examples, shows how to integrate this approach into rounds.

Similarly, the beginning intern will be well served by reviewing Chapter 4, "The On-Call Time," prior to internship (and perhaps again after several weeks). The increased independence, responsibility, and confidence you have will be the reward for the long hours of being on call. Dr. Hammad provides important tips on how to maximize the educational and patient care aspects of on-call time (while still getting some sleep).

Chapter 5 provides a guide to common patient problems that you will be asked to evaluate. For each problem a framework for analysis is outlined that will be a valuable reference to be rapidly reviewed prior to seeing the patient. This section will be repeatedly pulled from your lab coat and used throughout internship.

Dr. Hammad provides insightful analysis of the challenges facing the new house officer and simple, practical strategies to master them. Like a skilled and generous resident, this book provides essential information about how to be a successful intern and maximize the learning opportunities of internship. The title *Blackwell's Survival Guide for Interns* may be a bit misleading. This text will be extremely useful for third and fourth year medical students, as well as all disciplines of house officers working in the hospital setting.

David C. Tompkins, M.D.
Associate Chair of Medicine
Director of Student Programs
Department of Medicine
Health Sciences Center—Stony Brook

Preface

The time prior to commencing internship is a time when a medical student is most anxious. He or she wonders: what if I don't know something? What if a patient codes? What if I mess up? Are people going to be nice to me? How should I behave around them? *Blackwell's Survival Guide for Interns* is written to prepare interns mentally and intellectually for their internship. It contains everything an intern needs to do or not do to make internship more efficient, enjoyable, and the best learning experience possible. This book is written to help interns be the best they can be during the most difficult year of their career. The book's intention is not to make internship appear easy, but to show interns what they may realistically expect and then mentally prepare them to deal with it.

The introduction of the book contains several excerpts from my personal journal, which I wrote after my first 36 hours on-call (my second day of internship). These are true expressions of how I felt and are perhaps representative for most interns at the beginning of their internship.

Chapter 1 deals with many aspects of the internship that will inevitably affect your performance. Focusing on patient satisfaction as the primary goal of medicine, it teaches you how to optimize your resources and discusses how to interact with patients, their families, nurses, other interns, medical students, attending physicians, and other members of the health care team. The time management strategies presented are intended to ensure that your internship serves as an effective cornerstone for your medical education. Finally, Chapter 1 discusses personal issues that might affect an intern's performance.

Chapter 2 contains the results of two surveys given to members of a typical health care team, including patients. From them, you will learn what each discipline seeks in an intern and how you may best meet these expectations by balancing your efforts holistically. The ultimate goal of this chapter is to examine what turns a good doctor into a great one.

Chapter 3 discusses a new trend in health care—evidenced-based medicine. It gives step-by-step instructions on how to utilize this approach in your practice. Again, effectively utilizing all available resources in this way enhances patient care.

Chapter 4 deals with the experience of being "on call." Because of the unique responsibilities associated with this duty, your time must be organized differently so as to give efficient and appropriate care. This chapter also discusses sleep management for the intern.

Chapter 5 focuses on the most common problems faced by most interns. It offers practical tips for dealing with "stat" situations. This chapter does not provide an exhaustive discussion of diseases and treatments, but rather suggests a "how to" strategy for facing these episodes with a minimum of trepidation.

Chapter 6 briefly summarizes the preceding chapters and offers general advice on how to thrive during your internship.

Mustafa Hammad

Acknowledgements

I owe a great deal of gratitude to my friend and colleague, Guadalupe Macias, MD, for her help with the surveys and support throughout writing this book. I would like to thank all patients, nurses, medical students, interns, residents and attendings that completed the surveys included in Chapter 2. A special note of thanks to the nurses at the University Hospital, Stony Brook for helping me (and many of my colleagues) throughout internship and residency. I am very thankful to Alison Seale, RN, Joseph Crimi, Laith Altaweel, MD, Barry Goats, MD, Michael Connolly, MD, and Elena Kaznatcheeva, MD, for their review of the manuscript and feedback. I wish to thank David C. Tompkins, MD, (Associate Chair of Medicine; Director of Student Programs; Department of Medicine Health Sciences Center – Stony Brook) for his feedback and writing the foreword. I also would like to thank Richard Barnet, MD, (Director of Residency Program; Department of Medicine Health Sciences Center – Stony Brook) for his support and guidance. Special thanks to Harry Hauca, RN, for his help with this book. Last and not least, I would like to extend special thanks to the editors at Blackwell Science: Beverly Copland, Amy Nuttbrock, Shawn Girsberger, Irene Herlihy, David Barnes, and Jill Hobbs for their support and help in bringing this project to the market.

Mustafa Hammad

Introduction

It is 6 A.M. I am in a strange, clattering hospital, standing by the nurses' station where charts are being flung about as the night shift prepares to close out. A nurse eyes me warily and then goes off with a unit of blood in her hand. Call bells are going off as another nurse goes to respond; a dietitian is flipping through a chart and muttering to herself. The only thing I can think of is "controlled chaos." I had already been given my assignment: 12 patients—2 of whom were new, which implied that the other 10 had significant conditions requiring extended hospital stays. The list is crumpled somewhere in my starchy white coat. It wouldn't be too bad but I feel so conspicuous as I begin to go looking for the patient charts. The patients were being cared for by another intern (now a resident) who left off-service notes that were inadequate and poorly assembled. As a result, I am forced to go through each patient's chart to gain an appropriate understanding of his or her condition. My clinical misgivings are compounded by my feelings of isolation and loneliness. I have many "colleagues" around me, but don't *know* a single person, let alone consider those people to be my equals. The physical tolls of my new endeavor are quickly apparent, as I missed breakfast; I am famished and this is only the first day!

Now comes the task of finding the charts. The first two are found quickly, and I tuck them under my arm and begin to go to the doctor's room when a nurse stops me. "Just take one chart at a time. I have to chart on both of them." So I go back with one chart. There is another intern in the room already. She is flipping the pages and writing notes with grim ferocity. We nod to one another, and I pull up a chair and begin taking my own notes, equally grim. Discharge rounds start at 9 A.M., and I have 12 patients—12 lives to review and countless decisions to make. Back and forth to the chart racks, trying to balance my time appropriately. Breakfast trays are being distributed as nurses and residents greet one another; a nurse corners a resident to discuss some IV orders in a heated fashion. No one walks slowly.

My shared office becomes decidedly close as it fills with more people. I can no longer write my notes while sitting, so I go to the nurses' station and manage to find a small corner of desk with a chair. I am oblivious to time—I know only that I don't have too much of it. My stomach growls and I regret not having eaten breakfast. Coffee would help, but I don't know where the cafeteria is. The resident finds me, introduces himself, and asks me how I'm doing. I lie and tell him "fine" as he walks away with a grin.

Once the relevant information is extracted from the charts, the anxiety of participating in my first rounds begins to take hold. Discharge rounds are started, and all of a sudden the previous three hours of reading seem futile. The rounds are performed by the attending physician, the resident, myself, another intern, a care coordinator, a social worker, the head nurse, and two medical students. The care coordinator leads the rounds, and discharge plans for each patient are discussed.

All of a sudden I am struck with the realization that I recall nothing about the patients. I have some papers with lab values scrawled, names, diagnoses—but I know nothing! Diaphoretic? No, it is sweat, pure and simple. When asked about my prospective course of treatment, I am hesitant as my doubts and fears are recycled. The team watches my discomfiture with silence. The resident graciously answers the bulk of the questions with the utmost professionalism. Although his concise, effective responses are impressive, the manner in which he handles them is even more admirable. The answers are given in such a manner that not only treats the questions posed, but saves me from embarrassment and humiliation. To this day I remain in his debt. The team condenses its recommendations and slowly comes to a conclusion on the most appropriate discharge protocol. Although I have not performed as I would have liked, I learn a great deal and am relieved that the rounds are finished.

The attending physician then leads his rounds and I am fortunate in that his expectations of me are somewhat more realistic. Once again, the resident fields the majority of the questions while allowing for my input when appropriate. With rounds completed, it is time to review orders with my resident and discuss treatments and protocols.

Just finding where things are located proves to be a challenge. Name tags help me to associate names with faces, as introductions come quickly. Lunch is out of the question as I pore through charts, attempting to get as much insight as possible. Now that I am the intern of record, the nurses feel free to bombard me with questions for which I have no answer—not because I am incompetent, but because I am *new*. My ignorance of hospital protocol is hardly ever met with sympathy. The nurses with whom I work have their own issues, and I regret the fact that my ignorance is burdensome. Sometime during that afternoon I am actually able to meet patients directly, but I feel in a sort of fog as names, faces, diagnoses, and treatments are not yet imprinted on my consciousness.

The beeper, pager, or whatever you call it is an electronic torture device disguised in the garb of progress. It is a tormentor. It is an invisible shackle. It is the reincarnation of the grammar-school bully. It is a sad necessity and I have come to hate it. From the moment I enter the doors until the time I leave, this electronic chain jerks me away from whatever I am doing. The constancy of the pages makes completing any patient care nearly impossible, but each page has to be answered.

Dinner comes and goes, and I think that at this rate I will shed those few extra pounds that have plagued me since pre-med. Maybe I will write a diet book and never have to look for another chart that has found its way to CT scan. The day shift leaves and the evening nurses come on—more introductions, more questions, more sweat. My first day is coming to a grateful end as I retreat to a corner, and begin to write progress notes on my 12 patients. Hungry and both emotionally and physically spent, I leave the hospital at 10:30 P.M. and begin my one-hour commute. It is one of life's small miracles that my nodding off behind the wheel does not become something more than terrifying.

I lie in my bed with thoughts swirling around and around. Why did I want to become a doctor? Will each day be as bad as this one? Have I made the right decisions regarding my patients? I never thought my internship would be this difficult. Could I handle this job for a full year? It has been only one day, but I've already thought about quitting four times. As destructive as this experience is physically, the emotional challenge is tenfold greater. Four more years at this pace is ludicrous. I have never doubted the degree to which I enjoy helping people, but at what expense? My happiness? My health? My sanity? I used to think I entered this field for the lifestyle, but I could live comfortably on a "9 to 5" job and invest *far* less academically and mentally. I would be fooling myself if I claimed to know the answers to questions as intimate as these—all I know is that I will come to work each day and will slog along this most challenging path. Regardless of what makes me pursue medicine, I know the end result of my labors will culminate in a gift that is exhilarating and intangible. Sleep, when it comes, is deep and dreamless.

The second day includes an overnight call. I had thought this day would be better (I have found where to get coffee and have eaten breakfast) and worse (now a regular, I am supposed to know everything). Rounds are a blur, my resident is not as deft in giving responses as yesterday, charts are impossible to find, and a nurse pulls me aside to go over orders which, when I review them, make little sense. It is my second day, but I face the sorrow of pronouncing my first patient dead and breaking the news to her family. That night I realize a brutal fact: There is no adjustment period for an intern. The only thing more demanding than my patients' conditions is the idea that I don't have any time to make a *transition* into being a doctor—I already am one!

My call starts at 5 P.M., when everyone signs out their patients to me. There are many labs, X rays, and CT scans to check. A few patients are critical, and I have to check on them throughout the night. All patients become my immediate responsibility because I am THE DOCTOR. The patients are spread over 6 floors and 12 units. I begin rounding on them almost immediately, hoping that nothing acute will happen during the night. Prioritizing the patients makes this process simpler, as the most serious receive most of my attention. The one good thing about the off-tour hours is the presence of fewer people. Oh, everyone remains busy and intense, but there is less noise and fewer distractions—jokes are possible. The nurses, I discover, hold no personal grudges against me; they just want me to ask for some of their coffee instead of simply taking it. I am becoming more familiar with my own patients and comfortable with their treatments. The resident drops by to see how I am faring and give some last-minute instructions before heading out. For all intents and purposes I am now flying solo—or so I think.

My night is spent being excessively cautious; "Do no harm" becomes my mantra. I ramble among the units and fret over the charts, hoping no one becomes critical. I walk by a room where a patient is watching one of the popular doctor shows. Right. The night wears on uneventfully but I am never bored; I become more uptight as the sky lightens.

After being up all night answering numerous pages, I begin rounding on my team's patients at 5 A.M. I have to know all 28 of them, because neither my co-intern nor resident is working that day. To make matters worse, because it is a weekend, the team attending physician is a covering physician, which means that he knows little about the team's patients and that it is *my* responsibility to keep him informed. By the time I finish seeing the patients, I am exhausted; not only am I thorough, but I am also excessively cautious. The attending comes late, is unbearably slow that morning, and is oblivious to the fact that I have been on call the previous night. My eyes are half-closed. Although I am aware of how unprofessional I appear, my body won't compromise. I avoid food once again on Saturday and am content with Friday evening's dinner, which consisted of a doughnut supplied by one of the more sympathetic nurses.

The rounds are finished at 3 P.M. Fear and doubt leave as I am now officially relieved. The only task before me is charting on all 28 patients. I am tired—no, beyond tired. I am drained and devoid of energy. My charting is completed by 6 P.M. I am feeling angry—angry at the long night, at the nurses, and at my choice of profession. Exhausted, I toy with the idea of sleeping in my car. Another small miracle as I make it home again. I arrive home from my first 36-hour shift at 7 P.M. This time I lie in bed, seething with rancor against my medical school . . . it had not prepared me for this "being a doctor" stuff!

I collapse on my bed until 2 P.M. the following afternoon. My weekend is ruined but I still enjoy my Sunday as I idle on the couch, wondering what tomorrow will bring. I don't need to go out and have fun, but only to mentally brace myself for tomorrow's insanity. Doubt and fear have their arms around my shoulders all day, as I think constantly about what tomorrow will bring.

*****

I wrote those words in a journal that I began shortly after commencing my internship. Being an intern is the most unique and challenging experience I have ever faced. Having met with many doctors over the course of my career, I can safely say that my feelings are not unique. With the confidence of numbers, I can state that your internship will be one of the most difficult—and rewarding—periods of your personal and professional life. The purpose of this book is not to relate my own experiences as an intern, but to decrease your difficulty and maximize the rewards you receive by facing this challenge.

It is inevitable that an intern will adjust eventually to the new situation with the help of his or her preceptor. Although an intern may not be able to control the volume of calls, patients, or pages, he or she can learn to maximize the resources available and work efficiently. Not everyone makes it through the internship, but a few weeks' experience will give most interns a good idea of whether they will make it. You will eventually become more comfortable in this unique environment and be able to focus more intently on patient care.

The thanklessness of your efforts as an intern will amplify your struggles, and one can merely pray that he or she is coupled with a resident who is willing to offer sufficient patience and guidance. Of the hundreds of people with whom I worked during my internship, the resident was the one who consistently showed some understanding and compassion. Perhaps because the hardships of his internship were so fresh in his mind, he counseled me and became an integral part of my medical training. He answered any clinical questions, when possible, and allowed me the time needed to adjust to hospital life without getting upset at my slow pace. Residents may not have as much clinical knowledge as attending physicians, but their value to a new intern is unparalleled.

You may want to quit. You will likely be fatigued for so long that it will seem natural (doesn't everyone fall asleep leaning against an elevator wall?). Frustration will become your bread and butter as friends and family members see the new you. In the past, you may have been the most caring and compassionate individual in the world. You may have cared for the poor and loved puppies—but not any more. Like a soldier in combat, you will adapt to your new environment and find yourself changing. Can you be compassionate after sleeping for less than 1 hour in the last 36? Where is your kindness when you tell someone that he or she will shortly die? Can you maintain your composure as a drunk, fragrant with alcohol, curses you? Yes, you can. Above all, can you deal with the loneliness? For you will most certainly be alone, as few can or will relate to your problems and woes.

As an intern, you may feel that you are the only provider who is enduring hardships. In reality, the stress of patient care is distributed throughout the medical hierarchy. Everyone—from residents and nurses, to attending physicians and administrators—is overwhelmed. Everyone in the hospital is nervous about the first few weeks of internship, not just you. The resident is worried about getting a weak intern who might need constant reinforcement and baby-sitting. The nurses are nervous because they know that new interns will make many errors that could jeopardize patient care. The attendings are even more nervous, because they will bear the ultimate responsibility for patient care, including correcting your mistakes. You will not gain overnight popularity.

Have faith in yourself, your choices, your abilities, your religion, and the notion that you will eventually adjust to such a rigorous lifestyle. Some people may take longer than others to adapt to the new conditions, but that delay does not present a real problem. Ultimately, time is both a friend and an enemy. With time comes confidence and self-assurance, as what was improbable yesterday becomes routine today. This transformation *will* happen, and you will make it happen.

Blackwell's Survival Guide for Interns is intended to prepare you for your first year. It includes do's and don'ts, advice, and reflections. Many of its recommendations may seem to be simply common sense, but unfortunately stress can often make even the most rational person less than logical.

The book is centered on both efficiency and interaction. Chapter 1 deals with many aspects of the internship that will inevitably affect your performance. It teaches you how to optimize your resources and reminds you that patient satisfaction is the primary goal of medicine. It discusses how to interact with patients, their families, nurses, other interns, medical students, attending physicians, and other members of the health care team. It describes time management strategies intended to ensure that your internship serves as an effective cornerstone for your medical education. Finally, Chapter 1 discusses personal issues that might affect an intern's performance.

Chapter 2 contains the results of two surveys given to members of a typical health care team, including patients. From them, you will learn what each discipline seeks in an intern and how you may best meet these expectations by balancing your efforts holistically. The ultimate goal of this chapter is to examine what turns a good doctor into a great one.

Chapter 3 discusses a new trend in health care—evidenced-based medicine. It gives step-by-step instructions on how to utilize this approach in your practice. Again, effectively utilizing all available resources in this way enhances patient care.

Chapter 4 deals with the experience of being "on call." Because of the unique responsibilities associated with this duty, your time must be organized differently so as to give efficient and appropriate care. This chapter also discusses sleep management for the intern.

Chapter 5 focuses on the most common calls faced by most interns. It offers practical tips for dealing with "stat" situations. This chapter does not provide an exhaustive discussion of diseases and treatments, but rather suggests a "how to" strategy for facing these episodes with a minimum of trepidation.

Chapter 6 gives a brief summary of the preceding chapters and overall advice on how to thrive through internship.

1

The Internship Synopsis

THE PURPOSE OF INTERNSHIP

J. W. Hurst has described the purpose of internship as the study of human behavior (including that of the interns) and ways to do medicine (1). To see why this study is so important, consider the analogy of a car. You can learn all about the principles of the internal combustion engine. You can study the rules of the road and applicable laws for every state. You can delve into the physics of moving bodies. But guess what? You still won't know anything about driving a car.

In much the same way, medical schools do not prepare students for doctoring. They may excel in teaching both didactic and clinical medicine, but do they really prepare students psychologically for treating patients? They generally fail to instruct would-be physicians in situational or crisis management and provide little integration of medical knowledge with skills, patient care, or daily routines. In reality, an enormous gulf separates the processes of making a diagnosis based on test results and diagnosing the 67-year-old man in front of you with cancer. Medical schools may teach students how to treat the disease, but they rarely touch on treating the patient or interacting with the patient's family. This chapter endeavors to unify the knowledge you have with a feasible plan of patient care that

1

will enhance your practice and improve the quality of care that you provide.

Think of yourself as a new person as you enter your internship. Whatever prejudices you may have possessed—lose them. Those annoying personal habits you have cherished for all these years—forget them. Now is the time to reinvent a new and better you. Your internship offers an opportunity to become the person you have always longed to be. You can forge a revised and unique you that will envelope your personal life and professional career. You can take those didactic skills learned in medical school and slowly bind them with the traits that make a great doctor.

This passage will not be an easy feat—nor is it meant to be. The transition from medical student to intern is both abrupt and stressful. If you can accept and embrace that transformation, your chances for success will increase. Be deliberate as you practice, accept defeats, learn from the experience, and move forward, no matter how much you want to curl into a ball and cry. You'll do all right.

KEY POINTS

1. Learn patient care, not just knowledge.
2. Develop the unique you.
3. Use didactic skills learned in medical school and bind them with the traits that make a great doctor.
4. Learn from your experience.

COMPASSION

Compassion is one of the primary reasons that physicians should choose their profession. Without it, patients might as well receive treatment from a computer. Compassion is that singular quality that encompasses patience and tolerance—qualities that you may be hard-pressed to find during moments of fatigue and stress. Regardless, it is never appropriate to forget compassion's significance. As strung out as you may become, it is imperative that you place the needs of your patients first. A newly diagnosed diabetic who recalls how his mother underwent a leg amputation may become bitter and hostile—he has every right to feel this way. This patient does not care that you have notes to write or that you have worked seven days in a row. His only thoughts center on himself and his disease; yours should, too. He may blame you for his condition and irrationally attack you for being a poor physician. Where is your compassion? Can you hold on to it? Can you place yourself in his shoes?

A disease state is a stressful experience that is exacerbated by being in a hospital, a site where privacy, friends, and control are rare. Some people handle this situation well, whereas others do not. It is vital that you bear these facts in mind as you engage your patients in face-to-face encounters. Respect their fears and discomfort and acknowledge them. If they abuse you verbally, you must understand and know that they are not always this way; instead, their reaction to stress makes them behave in such an unpleasant way. You must not let their stress increase your own.

The ability to be compassionate with patients will carry over to your personal life as well. If you can be tolerant and understanding in a clinical setting, how much more benign will you be with friends and family? This strong foundation will enable you to build a character highlighted by grace and dignity. You can become a better person as well as a better doctor.

A compassionate physician places the needs of the patient first. As elementary as this idea may seem, rest assured that this tenet is often forgotten. Remind yourself that without the patient, there would be no need for you. Regardless of what you are doing, patient care should always be your first priority. Is the patient experiencing pain? Put yourself in his or her shoes before going for that cup of coffee. Pain management may not be as critical as an impending cardiac arrest, but it should nevertheless be a priority. After all, you are ultimately responsible for the quality of care given to your patient. Of course, it is impossible to be there every moment for your patient, but sometimes performing an advocate's role with other members of the health care team can make your job easier and the patient's lot more tolerable. The patient places his or her trust in you, a complete stranger: Take this trust and hold it responsibly and with dignity. Should you lose this trust, it may prove impossible to retrieve.

Take the time to listen to your patient. Your willingness to listen turns him or her into a member of your team and allows both of you to gauge the effectiveness of the current treatment. The act of listening serves many functions, not least of which is learning whether your patient suffers from depression. Depression can manifest itself quickly and immediate intervention for it—in the form of a psychiatric consult—should be forthcoming. In addition, listening allows you to discover things that might have been missed during the initial assessment but that may change the course of treatment.

It is interesting to discover how patients feel about those treating them. Chapter 2 describes the results of one such survey. In this study, what was paramount in patients' minds was not the amount of knowledge shown, but the degree to which compassion and manners were displayed—that is, the physician's demeanor. Even more astounding was that only 26% of the patients felt that strong medical knowledge alone made for a good doctor. This finding implies that your sound training must be combined with a pleasing manner to achieve success as a doctor, at least from the patient's perspective. As many physicians are extremely competent, it is your compassion for your fellow humans that will set you apart.

> To care and not know is dangerous. To know and not care
> is even worse. Caring and knowing must be combined to
> succeed in doctoring (1).

While showing compassion is critical, it is important to maintain a fine line that keeps you separate from your patients. Becoming too emotionally involved will result in an inability to function both professionally and personally. It is essential to maintain a working doctor–patient relationship; to do otherwise is to invite chaos and ruin.

A friend of mine, one whom I greatly admire and respect, was once caught up in this emotional quagmire. While caring for a terminally ill patient, she would call me in tears, sobbing about how poorly he was doing and how worthless she felt. At one point in her internship, she collapsed on the floor, distraught when a patient died. She communicated her feelings of worthlessness and failure as a result of not being able to intervene successfully. Although she is one of the most caring people I have ever met, such an approach to medicine can be highly detrimental. This physician treated each patient as a family member and thus reacted to illness with the most personal sensitivity. She was an asset to the medical community as a clinician, but her career would have been a short one had she continued along this path. Her emotional involvement began to take its toll at home as she brought her frustrations with her while off the job. Gradually, she managed to separate herself from her patients' conditions while maintaining the same excellent care she has always practiced. Today, she has reached a point where the major investment she makes in her patients is a professional one instead of a deeply personal one. That is, she has learned control and balance.

KEY POINTS

1. Compassion is one of the primary reasons physicians choose their profession.
2. Place the needs of your patients first.
3. A disease state is a stressful experience that can be exacerbated by being in a hospital.
4. Respect your patients' fears and discomfort and acknowledge them.
5. Take the time to listen to your patients.
6. "To care and not know is dangerous. To know and not care is even worse. Caring and knowing must be combined to succeed in doctoring" (1).

7. It is essential to maintain a working doctor–patient relationship.

THE PATIENT'S FAMILY

Remember what was said earlier about treating the patient and not just the illness? The patient is usually accompanied by his or her family, and you must deal with those individuals as well. Although not physiologically wanting, family members can become as burdensome as the patient as they try to cope with this stressor on family life. On the other hand, families can become a true asset to the physician; after all, they have extensive knowledge of the patient's habits and life patterns. You must therefore win them over to your side, by showing your compassion for them and for the patient. Become involved with family members, show them that you care, and respect them. Remind them of their important role in the healing process. Obtaining their assistance will make your treatment plan more effective and your life easier.

Demonstrate your concern to family members by staying in touch with them; update them frequently and let them know what you are doing for their family member. Working in this manner, you can turn the family into allies, rather than liabilities. Never rely on someone else to talk to them—do it yourself. Of course, not all families will respond as you would like. Remember, however, that you are not engaging in a pure science. The variables of human behavior are inherent in the profession you have chosen.

Keep the family informed of any changes in the patient's condition, both good and bad. Make sure that they understand the whys and wherefores of the treatment by couching your explanations in language that they can understand. Always document your actions—for example, by writing "patient family informed" or "discussed with patient and his family" in the patient's record. It is also a good idea to let your resident or attending physician discuss a serious diagnosis with the patient and his or her family.

KEY POINTS

1. Families can be a true asset to the physician, as they have extensive knowledge of the patient's habits and life patterns.
2. Get family members on your side.
3. Show them your compassion and respect.
4. Stay in touch with them and update them frequently.

DIFFICULT PATIENTS

We all have bad days. On some days, all you can do is smile and fake it. Imagine that, on your day off, the chief resident pages you and asks you to cover for an ill colleague. You cannot say "no" because you are the first back-up. What makes the situation more galling is that you are covering for someone whom you do not particularly like. You are certain that her illness is a sham. You feel annoyed and persecuted. A bird blesses you as you stalk to your car.

You reach the hospital and notify the operator that you will be covering for Dr. Have-a-headache; he smiles apologetically as a code is called. The issues between the pager and yourself intensify as you are called for the most mundane things: Mr. S is constipated. Mrs. Y has a finger stick of 70; should the insulin be held? And then a tough one—a patient is throwing soda cans at everyone. First bird crap and now this.

What do you do? Do you see patients in your current agitated state, or do you calm down a bit first? The irate patient's condition is not life-threatening, so you opt for the calm-down route. You weasel a cup of coffee from one of the nurses as you once again regret entering this field, then walk slowly, perhaps chatting with someone as you head toward the disruptive patient. You maintain deep, steady breaths as you walk into his room.

Mr. T is an AIDS patient with extensive Kaposi's sarcoma and his world is fractured. He knows that he is dying and is dying alone, as his friends and family have abandoned him. He is angry with himself for the choices he has made. He is angry with his family. How do you react?

When faced with this situation, I slid a chair over to the bed and we talked—that's all, just talked. Although Mr. T felt better knowing that he was not abandoned by his caregivers, it was I who truly felt better. Although I had experienced a bad day, he made me realize just how fortunate I was. I would be leaving the hospital in a few hours to be with friends and family; I was in good health. Mr. T and so many others were considerably less lucky. I was reasonably sure of being alive tomorrow. Mr. T appreciated the time that I spent with him; he calmed down and eventually went to sleep. We parted better men.

Even though you may be having a bad day, it is important to recognize that ill people may not be in their normal emotional state. They and their families may seem hostile, nervous, or organically aggressive. The most well-mannered person may become transformed into a spiteful, mean-spirited, and abusive virago. Medicine is all about dealing with sick people under stress; you must treat their attitudes as well as their ailments.

Some patients may become overwhelmed at the news that they are gravely ill or dying. In such cases, you may have to dig down deep within yourself to reach their level of feeling. Show them that you truly care; break down the barrier that normally separates patient and doctor and simply listen. Therapeutic listening enables you to play the role of doctor, therapist, and psychologist simultaneously. Some patients may merely want someone to talk with them; others may be at the other end of the spectrum.

In spite of your best efforts, some patients will remain abusive and demanding. It is in these cases that you have an opportunity to excel. Be professional. Never raise your voice. The louder they scream, the calmer you should become. If you yell back, you merely feed their agitation. If they call you a "worthless, ignorant SOB," excuse yourself and walk calmly out of the room. Some patients will even expose themselves—be calm and gently leave. You may be seething inside, ready to burst. Nevertheless, it is important to maintain a calm demeanor. If you find the situation impossible, ask your resident or attending for assistance.

KEY POINTS

1. Ill people may not be in their normal emotional state.
2. You must treat patients' attitudes as well as their ailments.
3. Show them that you truly care.
4. Break down the barrier that normally separates patient and doctor and simply listen.
5. Be professional.
6. Never raise your voice.
7. If you find the situation impossible, ask your resident or attending for assistance.

BREAKING BAD NEWS TO PATIENTS

Most residents and attending physicians are the ones who deliver hurtful news to patients and families. Sometimes, however, this sad task falls to the intern, such as when a patient dies in the middle of the night.

If you are delivering the news to family members in person, following a few guidelines may help. Keep the conversation private. Never deliver the news in a hallway; instead, find a room where privacy can be obtained. Offer patients and their family members chairs on which to sit. If they prefer to stand, then you should stand as well. Try to keep your eyes level with theirs and maintain eye contact throughout. Briefly review the circumstances involved with the death. For example, explain that "Your mother was admitted for such and such, and we have done our best to treat her. But I am sorry to say that she passed away." Try to stay with the individuals for a few minutes and ask whether they have any questions or need any help. They may scream or become angry—be compassionate. Treat them as you would like to be treated under similar circumstances. If they become violent, leave the room.

Follow the same principles when dealing with patients. Try to stay at the patient's level and maintain eye contact. Explain the circumstances surrounding the hospitalization and illness very clearly. Ascertain that the patient understands his or her illness and the actions that have been taken thus far. Go over currently available treatment options. Be compassionate and understanding at all times as you speak in a low but not ominous tone of voice. Don't leave the room until all questions have been answered and you are certain the patient understands everything you have told him or her. It is far better to show your concern verbally rather than physically.

KEY POINTS

1. Deliver bad news in private—never in a hallway.
2. Offer family members a place to sit; if they prefer to stand, then you should stand as well.
3. Try to keep your eyes level with the other person's and maintain this eye contact throughout.
4. Speak in a low but not ominous tone of voice.
5. Briefly review the circumstances involved with the death or disease.
6. Try to stay with patients and their families for a few minutes and ask whether they have any questions or need any help.
7. Be compassionate. Treat them as you would like to be treated under similar circumstances.

HISTORY TAKING AND PHYSICAL EXAM

One of the first principles learned in medical school is that 85% of the diagnoses come from a good history and physical exam (H&P). This rule will stand for the rest of your career. The more time you spend obtaining a good H&P, the less money is spent making a diagnosis and the sooner proper treatment can begin.

Take a detailed history and do your own thorough

physical exam of each of your patients at least once at the time of admission. You might be surprised at the inaccuracies in the resident's report; the patient might have been the resident's third admission and the H&P might have been obtained at 4 A.M. Under these circumstances, faulty assessments can easily occur. For instance, I once had a patient who was admitted to my service with syncope. According to the H&P documentation, the patient didn't have bruits. When I examined the patient, however, I found that he had significant bilateral bruits. Perhaps the resident failed to listen to the patient's neck or perhaps he failed to hear the bruits. In any event, this finding changed the investigation of the syncope and the course of therapy.

Another example involved a patient with a history of coronary artery disease who was admitted to telemetry to rule out myocardial infarction (MI). As documented by the admitting resident, the reason for admission was an episode of nausea and light-headedness but no chest pain. When I assumed care for the patient the following morning, I took my own history and did my own physical exam. The patient revealed that he felt nauseated the night before admission after eating three hot dogs. The light-headedness occurred the following morning when he took his daily dose of Xanax. If this history had been obtained at the time of admission, the patient might not have been admitted. MI was ruled out in this case, and the patient was shortly discharged. This history changed the way in which the attending physician dealt with the case. It also illustrates how taking your own history can change the course of an admission.

A third example that clearly shows the crucial nature of a good H&P was described by one of my attendings. A 22-year-old female presented to the emergency room (ER) complaining of a severe, throbbing headache. The patient was seen and examined by an ER resident, who documented a normal exam, determined the possible etiology to be migraine headache, and gave her a dose of Demerol, which relieved the headache. A week later, the patient returned to the ER with the same complaint. She was again given a dose of Demerol and discharged. Two weeks later, the same patient presented with the same headache. The ER attending physician requested a neurology consult during this visit. Although the attending neurologist found the neurological exam to be unremarkable, she could not appreciate any breath sounds on the right side of the chest. A chest X ray was ordered, which subsequently revealed a large lung mass extending throughout most of the patient's right lung. A CT scan of the head showed multiple, small metastases to the brain. Reviewing the records dating back to when the patient first presented four weeks earlier revealed that the ER resident documented a normal physical exam, including lung auscultation. Clearly, the resident must have failed to actually auscultate the lungs. She assumed that, because the patient was a young, apparently healthy female, her presenting illness must be a headache and she must have a normal lung exam. This example signifies the importance of taking a good H&P and documenting the correct information so as to protect yourself and possibly save a life.

Be organized in taking your H&P. Follow a specific order with both the history taking and the physical exam that ensures that you perform a complete review of systems. I find it helpful to start with the head and move downward, with both the history and the exam. Make sure that you perform a complete examination on every patient, especially during the initial contact. You can then focus on the system that pertains to the presenting illness. Even when you undertake an elective in a subspecialty, perform a complete H&P when the patient is first admitted to your service. Don't focus on just the system that pertains to your specialty and ignore the rest of the body. You may be surprised at what you learn.

Understand the pathophysiology of the physical signs you notice. This information will enable you to understand why the signs are present, and it makes the overall picture of the disease become clearer. Observe your resident and attending when they perform a physical exam, as it will allow you to verify that you have acquired the correct skills.

In addition, it provides opportunities to learn different examining styles, which can only sharpen your own mastery of the H&P even further.

KEY POINTS

1. Eighty-five percent of all diagnoses come from a good history and physical exam.
2. Always take your own H&P when a patient is assigned to you.
3. Be organized in taking your H&P, and follow a certain order when examining systems.
4. Understand the pathophysiology of the physical signs you notice.
5. Observe your resident and attending doing physical exams, and use these occasions to improve your skills or learn different styles of examination.

TEAMWORK

Taking care of a patient requires the efforts of an entire team of caregivers, not just the services of a single doctor. This team may include the patient and his or her family, the nurse, a social worker, a care coordinator, a physical therapist, the medical student, the intern, the resident, the attending physician, and other medical personnel. You should be the dynamic leader of the team. Everyone on the team should be your advisors—ask for their input at all times. Never hesitate to seek help from anyone you believe might know the answer to your question. The medical student should be your assistant as well as your student. Teach him or her how to follow in your footsteps once he or she becomes an intern. Never forget that the patient and family members are integral members of your team. Ultimately, the team's goal is enhanced patient care. Each member should know everything that is happening with the patient, including the patient.

As a leader, you assume the dynamic responsibility for

the patient. Your self-worth will increase as you gain the respect and trust of your teammates, including the patient. Your efforts guarantee that the patient will receive the best care possible. They also ensure that your internship experience will be more positive and worthwhile.

Teamwork requires you to help your fellow interns with their work when possible. If you have finished with your task, ask whether anyone else needs help. There is nothing wrong in helping nurses as they care for your patient; you'll earn both their respect and the respect of the patient. A thing as simple as holding a patient while a dressing is changed or cleaning up after you do a procedure can yield enormous benefits. Never leave your work for others. Instead, try to finish your work on your own. If you need help, however, ask for it.

KEY POINTS

1. Be the dynamic leader of the team.
2. Treat everyone else on the team as your advisor and ask for their input at all times.
3. Never hesitate to seek help.
4. Ask whether anyone else needs help.
5. Never leave your work for others.

NURSES

Nurses are among the most vital members of your team. Your relationship with them can make your internship either easy or difficult. And here's the funny thing: The choice of whether you have them on your side or against it is entirely up to you! In most cases, this relationship becomes established during the first few days of your internship.

Most physicians believe that they are superior to and know more than nurses. They believe that doctors should write orders and that nurses should follow those orders, word for word, without argument. These beliefs and attitudes create a barrier between nurses and doctors and produce tension, which can subsequently compromise patients' care. For their part, most nurses assume that doctors who hold these biases are arrogant and condescending.

No matter what the cause, never do anything that might jeopardize patient care. You have committed yourself to serve your patients under all circumstances, no matter the cost.

Without nurses, your job would be nearly impossible. Never underestimate how much nurses know, especially at the beginning of your internship. Even if you don't believe that they know more than you, recognize that their knowledge is different from yours. Nurses spend the most time of any team member with the patient, thus gaining significant insight into his or her condition. If you allow yourself to be open-minded, you may find that you gain invaluable knowledge from nurses. People sense how you feel about them. If nurses feel that you respect them, they respond by respecting you as well; they not only will be professional in their attitude, but also will try to make your job easier!

The following suggestions are geared toward helping you establish a better relationship with nurses. When you start each rotation, go to each nursing station and introduce yourself. This practice invites nurses to be your collaborators. I ask the nurses to call me by my first name when we communicate with one another, which removes another barrier between us and allows us to work at the same level. Most nurses will call you by your first name only among themselves, but will call you by Dr. X in front of the patient and his or her family. The philosophy behind this strategy is simple: Win the nurses' trust and respect, and turn them into partners. They will then feel that you are "one of them" and not segregated in a different group.

Always answer nurses promptly when they page you. They are busy people and don't have time to continually look for you. Imagine how frustrating it must be to page someone repeatedly and not receive an answer. Besides, your patient may be very ill and require your immediate attention. Nurses soon learn which interns answer in a timely fashion and which ones do not. If you are among the former group, they will understand when you can't answer immediately. They will assume that you are busy and won't bother to page you again until later. Furthermore, they won't page you unless the issue is truly important. If, on the other hand, you have a reputation for laxness in responding, nurses will page you repeatedly until you answer. They might even page your resident or attending—which will not look good at all.

Being among the doctors who answer pages quickly also pays off when you are on night call and in need of sleep. Nurses will understand your needs and will try not to call you unless it is absolutely necessary.

If a nurse asks you for a favor that will make his or her job easier, comply with the request as long as it does not compromise patient care. For instance, many times you will be asked to extend an intravenous line for 24 hours so that the nurse can change it a day later, especially if the patient is going to be discharged the following day. This practice does not put the patient at risk, but it does make the nurse's job easier. Don't order lab work at the change of the shift unless it is absolutely necessary. Doing so will keep nurses beyond their shift, which is not something that makes anyone happy. If an add-on blood draw can wait until the morning lab work, when the phlebotomist can handle it, then order it with the morning labs and don't make nurses do it separately. In this way, you help both the nurses and the patient, as the patient does not get stuck twice.

Always remember that nurses are part of your team, too. As a team player, you should strive to help all members in any way possible. If you display this courtesy, everyone will strive to make your job easier as well.

Nurses can teach you a great deal. They have more contact with your patients than you do. They have more experience than you do. They are more familiar with the environment in which you are working. Listen to and respect them. Acknowledge what they know and recognize that they are capable of helping you. Take advantage of their knowledge as much as possible. More importantly, teach them when you can. They are always eager to learn.

KEY POINTS

1. Never underestimate how much nurses know.
2. Introduce yourself when you first meet them.
3. Win their trust and respect, and turn them into partners.
4. Always answer nurses promptly when they page you.
5. If a nurse asks you for a favor that will make his or her job easier, comply with the request as long as it does not compromise patient care.
6. Nurses can teach you a great deal, so listen to them.

CONFIDENCE

Confidence is an essential requirement for a doctor. Doctors are in control of the most precious thing in the world, a human life. To show everyone, including your patient, that you are capable of taking care of that life, you must come across as confident but not cocky. Confidence does not necessarily come from knowledge. It derives from your conduct around people and your bearing. Being self-assured gains the trust and respect of those around you.

To exude confidence, you must be well read but not necessarily a know-it-all. Having good self-esteem requires that you have enough faith in your skills to admit that your knowledge may be limited. Confidence means that you are able to ask a question when appropriate. When someone asks you what to do in a certain patient care situation and you don't know, admit that fact. You can ask the other person for his or her thoughts on the matter and, if the two of you remain unsatisfied, look for another solution. To be confident means never giving an answer unless you are 100% sure of its accuracy, especially if it pertains to patient care, and showing others that you are comfortable with your knowledge and are not hesitant to gain more.

Patients place their lives in your hands. Make them feel that they have made the right choice. When doing a procedure or recommending a treatment, know what you are talking about. If a patient asks for your opinion about a treatment and you have no experience with the therapy, explain that you are not familiar with it but will investigate it and report back to him or her. By showing your honesty in this way, your patient is more likely to trust you in other matters.

KEY POINTS

1. Demonstrate your confidence without being cocky.
2. Confidence does not necessarily come from knowledge.
3. Be well read but not necessarily a know-it-all.
4. Having good self-esteem means that you have enough faith in your skills to admit that your knowledge may be limited.
5. Be able to ask a question when appropriate.
6. Never give an answer unless you are 100% sure of its accuracy.

PROACTIVITY

One of the best books I have read and recommend to everyone is Stephen Covey's *The Seven Habits of Highly Effective People* (2). According to this book, the first habit of these highly effective people is proactivity. Covey states that effective people are proactive—not reactive to their environment. That is, they live according to their own internal values. You will be working with a variety of people every day during each rotation, so the likelihood that you will encounter difficult patients or team members is quite high. When faced with such a situation, you have two options: (1) react to the person's behavior, become frustrated, and learn to hate your job; or (2) live by your own standards and try to work through the experience while maintaining your integrity. That is, you can make the best of the situation and keep the patient your number one priority.

Know that there will be trying situations where you will be tempted to react with anger—but don't. Allow the other person to vent and express his or her anger and frustration. If you trust in who you are and feel comfortable with yourself, nothing the person says can harm you. The anger and arrogance shown by such an individual derive from that person's own insecurity and low self-esteem. Furthermore, no one can ever make you feel inferior without your cooperation.

KEY POINTS

1. Read *The Seven Habits of Highly Effective People* by Stephen Covey.
2. Be proactive—not reactive to your environment.
3. Live according to your own internal values.
4. Work through an experience with a difficult person while maintaining your integrity.
5. Don't react with anger.
6. No one can ever make you feel inferior without your cooperation.

SELF-RESPECT

To gain respect, you have to give it. This two-way street results in a more friendly environment, which in turn allows you to be more productive. No matter what you do, however, you will inevitably encounter people who are mean-spirited and disrespectful. They might scream at you, humiliate you, look down upon you, and use you. Some interns put up with this behavior and walk away intimidated.

Abusive people who act in such a way are insecure about themselves. They have weak self-esteem and try to feed on others' weakness to gain more strength for themselves. The more weakness you show, the more strength you give the abusive person, thereby allowing him or her to put you through an emotional wringer. Those interns who accept the humiliation will be treated that way repeatedly. Conversely, those who stand up for themselves will walk away with their self-respect intact.

Some interns become aggressive and vengeful toward people who humiliate them. These retaliatory responses are self-destructive. Remember your place in the pecking order and see the logic here. When push comes to shove, your superiors can essentially make you bear responsibility for anything that goes wrong.

You must be savvy in dealing with difficult people. If an individual raises his or her voice with you, don't scream back—it merely gives your opponent another reason to become louder. Instead, calmly and politely inform the person that you do not appreciate this sort of conduct. Tell him or her that if you did something wrong, you are sorry for it, but you don't deserve to be treated in this manner. Maintain your strong, steady stance. By doing so, you prevent the abusive person from feeding on your weakness, as you didn't reveal any openings. Along the way, you may gain some respect from your opponent. Of course you are a human who makes many mistakes—but that fact does not give anyone the right to belittle you. Do your best, do not be lazy, and respect others and yourself.

Anyone can have a bad day. Everyone reacts to adversity differently. Sometimes people who are not coping well will heap their frustrations on others unintentionally. If you know that the person who yelled at you is normally polite, be patient. He or she will probably come back and apologize for the bad behavior. Even our closest family members can act this way. If a patient treats you poorly, understand that the person is under stressors that he or she might not be able to bear. Be professional and polite, step out of the room, and come back later.

KEY POINTS

1. To gain respect, you have to give it.
2. Abusive people who act in a mean way are generally insecure about themselves.

3. Maintain a strong and steady stance when faced with difficult people.

YOUR FRIENDS AND FAMILY

There are times during your internship when you will become frustrated, hate your job, and want to quit. These "moments of insanity" will soon pass, however. Nevertheless, accept the fact that the lifestyle during internship is a difficult one. You work hard for long hours, for days on end. It is imperative that you have a friend at work who can relate to you and your problems. Early in your internship, try to find someone with whom you can form an open and honest relationship—someone who will allow you to blow off steam and be empathetic. Strengthen that relationship and use it to support one another through difficult times.

You should also have a friend outside of work with whom you can socialize—someone with whom you can goof off, so you can return to work a bit more relaxed on the following day. Ideally, that person will know nothing about the medical field and care little about the differences between a beta blocker and an ACE inhibitor. Let this friend remind you of your former life and the pleasures that the world has to offer.

Make sure you have "a life" outside work. Don't let your profession dominate your existence. If you do, you will become less productive, less efficient, and bored. You may also lose your family. Your attitude at work will affect your personal life, no matter how hard you try to prevent it from happening. If you are not happy with your job, you will not be happy at home. Try not to bring your work home, especially after a bad day. You can dedicate a few minutes to talk to your family about your trials, but then forget about your work problems and try to enjoy time together. Conversely, if you had a good day, share it with your family members so that they can relate to you.

Soon after you start your internship, you may notice

that your conversations with your friends and family tend to revolve around medical "crap." Your friends may insist that you stop talking about medicine so much. Your mind somehow becomes programmed to insert medical terms and topics into every conversation. You may not notice this tendency until someone tells you to stop talking medical garbage, finish your drink, and watch the game. Just pay extra attention to what you are saying and avoid mixing medical terms and patient stories in your normal conversation outside work.

Take time for yourself. Go to the gym as frequently as possible. It's a great way to relieve some of your stress as well as a good place to meet people. Try to eat healthy food and practice what you preach. It's difficult to eat well—if at all—on the job. Try to eat at least one nutritious meal at home. Try to get enough sleep, because adequate rest assures you of a healthier mind and body. Even while on call, if you get a chance to sleep, take it.

KEY POINTS

1. It is imperative that you have a friend at work who can relate to you and your problems.
2. Ideally, you should also have a friend outside of work with whom you can socialize.
3. Make sure you have "a life" outside work.
4. Try not to bring your work home, especially after a bad day.
5. Take time for yourself.
6. Go to the gym as frequently as possible.
7. Try to eat healthy food and practice what you preach.
8. Try to get enough sleep.

ORGANIZATION

Organization is a fundamental part of life. Organized interns are efficient and thorough, and they make fewer mistakes. Organization is a skill that, if mastered during internship, can be carried over the rest of your career. This section provides some tips for better organization during internship.

Write down everything that needs to be done. This practice can be a life saver when you have too many patients and too little time. For instance, if your attending asks you to order a magnetic resonance imaging (MRI) study before you discharge a patient and you don't write the order down, you are apt to forget it until the next day. This negligence will reflect poorly on you and will keep the patient in the hospital for another day. It also means that you must write another note on the patient. Keep in mind that the longer the patient stays in hospital, the greater his or her risk of contracting infection. Write down all lab work required for all patients every day before rounds. Having this information handy will make you look good in front of the resident or attending. Most importantly, you will rarely miss the opportunity to correct a lab value that might save a life.

Make a daily "to do list" for each patient and place a check mark next to an item when it is completed. At the end of the day, review your list to see what else needs to be done. Sometimes it's good to work hard for a couple of hours, so that a portion of the day is relatively free. Doing so guarantees complete and efficient patient care and helps you finish your day early (or at least on time).

In Stephen Covey's *The Seven Habits of Highly Effective People,* the third habit is time management (1). Covey introduces an effective way to organize one's day by dividing it into four quadrants:

- First quadrant: things that are important and urgent
- Second quadrant: matters that are important but not urgent
- Third quadrant: items that are not important but urgent
- Fourth quadrant: things that are not important and not urgent

23

You can use the same method to organize your day. The first quadrant might hold critical actions such as STAT orders, STAT discharge summaries, or starting medications on a patient. The second quadrant could include things that affect the long-term goals of your internship, such as educational schedules. For instance, you might write down the time for a lecture that day, a peripheral smear to be reviewed, an autopsy to watch, or a topic to look up on the Internet. The third quadrant can be used for things that are important to others but not to you, such as writing an evaluation for a medical student, calling a patient's family members and updating them on nonurgent issues, or helping your team members in their work. The fourth quadrant is reserved for items that are neither important nor urgent, such as reading a magazine, going to the call room to watch TV, or chatting with coworkers.

Covey suggests using different colors for each quadrant to highlight when an item is completed. At the end of the day, you can measure your efficiency by seeing how much color appears in each quadrant. The more color in the first and second quadrants, the more efficient you were. Following this technique allows you to prioritize your activities and measure the success of your planning.

Writing your daily progress notes early allows team members to read any new information pertaining to each patient. As your first activity in the morning, start a progress note for each patient assigned to you. Write the patient's name on the note, visit him or her, and record the patient's vital statistics. Then sit down and take a few minutes to document both the subjective and objective findings before starting your rounds. While rounding with the attending or shortly after, chart the assessment and plan. This strategy allows the team to find out the assessment and plan for each patient early during the day. It is also good for you to get things done and out of the way as soon as possible.

KEY POINTS

1. Write down everything that needs to be done for each patient.

2. Make a daily "to do list."
3. Read *The Seven Habits of Highly Effective People* and construct a four-quadrants day organizer.
4. Write daily progress notes early during the day.
5. Get things done and out of the way as soon as possible.

PRESENTATION

Gaining the trust and respect of the attending physician is essential to making your internship profitable. If the attending believes you are competent, reliable, and thorough, he or she will give you more autonomy. This independence allows you to relax, because you do not have to deal with being under constant observation. You may interact with the attending only during rounds. It is during this process that attendings form an opinion of you as you present your patients.

Several strategies may help improve your presentations. Be organized when you present each patient, keeping in mind the need for structure. Follow a certain format and apply it to every case. Each attending has a particular style in which he or she would like to hear the case. Learn that style and develop a format that suits the attending physician's preferences; then follow that format with each patient. Some attendings demand lengthy, detailed presentations, whereas others want the short version. Ask your resident which style the attending prefers for the presentation. In fact, you can ask the attending how the case should be presented.

Some attending physicians want to hear the chief complaint first; others need the past medical history first. Some want all information about the patient, including the complete H&P; others prefer to hear only the information pertaining to the presenting illness. Attendings might ask you to present in great detail, including a detailed exam, until they establish that you are competent and trust your abilities. Later, they might just require you to give just the most pertinent information about the patient.

Be confident when presenting the physical exam.

25

Never say, "I think I heard a murmur"; your statement should be either "I did hear a murmur," "I did not hear a murmur," "I didn't look for it," or "I am not sure." If you show hesitation, the attending will doubt your clinical skills and judgment. It is better to miss a finding because you didn't look for it than to miss it because you didn't know how to find it. If you heard a murmur, then say "I did hear it"—even if the attending does not. Remember, medicine is subjective and people can disagree about findings—whether an attending physician or an intern. If a murmur is important to the patient's presenting symptoms and you are not sure about hearing it, ask your resident to confirm what you did or did not find prior to making your presentation.

KEY POINTS

1. Be organized when you present.
2. Follow a certain format and apply it to every patient you present.
3. Learn each attending physician's preferred style of presentation and develop a format that suits each attending.
4. Be confident when presenting the physical exam.

DOCUMENTATION

Documentation, documentation, documentation. No one can overemphasize the importance of proper documentation. Your notes demonstrate your competency and confidence—or your lack of it. Documentation must be mastered during your internship because it will provide the patient with better care and protect you from legal action. If you train yourself to do this step well, it will pay off when you become an attending physician. Many people participate in the patient's care and the only way to communicate with them is through the chart. Everything you do for the patient should be written down so that others will know what has already been done. This section provides several guidelines that you can follow to ensure better documentation.

Write as legibly as you can. Writing an illegible note is equivalent to not writing it at all—if it can't be read, the information is useless. Write your note in an organized fashion so that someone can understand exactly what's going on with the patient and the plan of care. Always use black ink; it is more legible and, when photocopied, comes out clearer than red or blue ink. Definitely no writing with a pencil!

Documentation should include daily progress notes, discussions with the patient and his or her family, placement of IV lines, drawing of blood, consults, abnormal lab findings and steps taken to correct them, and any conversations held with anyone regarding the patient. Get into the habit of indicating that you discussed the case with the attending and resident, noting their names; just make sure that you really do discuss the case with them.

Write down information on a daily basis for each patient. The most important part of your note focuses on any changes in the pertinent physical exam and the assessment and plan. The assessment and plan is the part that is most frequently read by other members of your team. The basic principle in writing this section is to ensure that the reader learns what has been done thus far and what is being planned. It should be organized in a problem-based fashion, with each problem (including social issues) being noted separately. List your plan in working up each problem and explain how you are treating each issue. The problem list should include any inactive medical problems. Sometimes the plan for a particular problem may be unclear, so write down your logic and explain what conditions you are trying to rule out and what tests you are ordering to eliminate those possibilities.

As mentioned above, your notes reveal your level of competency. A good note should be thorough enough to address every problem and your action in dealing with it, yet brief enough that you don't repeat unchanged findings every day. Never parrot the notes of your attending or resident, even if you change some words around. You may discuss the case with the attending and resident prior to writing your note, but always write the thoughts on your own mind.

Print or stamp your name under your signature to ensure that people know who authored the note. If you are proud of your note, you will be proud to print your name underneath it. Never abbreviate words or terms, as some people might not understand the abbreviation (even if it's a commonly used one). Abbreviations can become dangerous if they are misinterpreted, especially in writing orders. Most institutions have their own lists of acceptable abbreviations, and you should always adhere to your particular institution's list.

KEY POINTS

1. Write as legibly as possible.
2. Write your note in an organized fashion.
3. Always use black ink.
4. Documentation should include daily progress notes, discussions with the patient and his or her family, placement of IV lines, drawing of blood, consults, abnormal lab findings and steps taken to correct them, and any conversations held with anyone regarding the patient.
5. Print or stamp your name under your signature.
6. Avoid using abbreviations.

EVALUATION

Evaluation is a feedback tool that should enhance your skills and learning. It is essential to learn how you are doing, so that you can target your weak areas for improvement. The best way to obtain feedback is to ask for it. Feedback should be given throughout the rotation by every member of the team—most importantly, by the patient. Make your teammates feel comfortable enough to give you an appraisal, good or bad, by asking them for it. By requesting feedback, you invite your team members to give you their honest opinions in a constructive manner. Seeking out their counsel also reveals that you are interested in becoming better at what you do and that you see their opinions as important.

Evaluations by attendings should be viewed not as a grading tool, but rather as a way to learn your weaknesses and strengths. It is recommended that you get feedback from your resident and attending at least three times during each rotation.

At the beginning of the rotation, ask your resident and attending about their requirements and the way in which they like to run things. You can then tailor your efforts to comply with their needs so that your job and theirs goes more smoothly. After a few days, ask the resident and the attending to evaluate you. Simply ask, "How am I doing?" or "Can you tell me how I have been doing so far?" By doing so, you can adjust your style to suit their needs and make sure that you are on the right track. It also shows the resident and attending that you are concerned and want to improve.

The second time to ask for feedback is the middle of the rotation. During the last two weeks of the rotation, you should be at your best so as to impress your attending and resident. Good performance at this point diminishes any mistakes you might have made during the first two weeks, as people will remember the last two weeks more than the first two.

The final evaluation and feedback should occur at the end of the rotation. Your performance should not be the focus of your evaluation, but rather should be seen as a way to improve in your next rotation and the rest of your career.

It is also essential to obtain feedback from your program director. Go to the office and ask to see the evaluations given by attendings and residents. Ask the program director for his or her own view of you as well. This information will fill in the whole picture for you. Remember, your ultimate goal should be to improve steadily throughout your internship and subsequent residency.

KEY POINTS

1. The best way to obtain feedback is to ask for it.
2. Evaluations by attendings should be considered a way to learn your weaknesses and strengths.
3. It is recommended that you seek feedback from your resident and attending at least three times during each rotation.
4. Get feedback from your program director at least once a year.
5. Your ultimate goal should be to improve steadily throughout your internship and subsequent residency.

DISCHARGE SUMMARIES

Discharge summaries are an intern's nightmare—a pain that no intern likes to endure. They are a time-consuming hindrance. Unfortunately, discharge summaries are part of your job description and are needed by the hospital for billing purposes and as part of the continuum of patient care. Discharge summaries are sent to the primary care doctor (PMD) after the patient's release to inform him or her of the patient's admission, matters that need to be followed up, and any changes in medications that occurred during the admission. Without the discharge summary, the PMD has no way of obtaining detailed information about the patient's admission. The discharge summary is also used in consecutive admissions. It gives the admitting physician a great deal of information about the patient, especially if the patient is a poor historian. So no matter how odious you find them, discharge summaries are essential.

How essential? Your privileges can be suspended for not dictating your discharge summaries in a timely fashion. You might receive one warning for your laxity, which is not a big deal. On the other hand, if your privileges are suspended, that fact will go on your permanent record and you will not be allowed to see patients until you are reinstated.

The following tips are intended to help you stay current with your dictations. First, always keep in mind that discharge summaries serve the best interests of your patient—which is why you entered this profession. Dictate the minute you discharge the patient. Actually, you should dictate immediately after you write the discharge orders and before returning the chart to the nurse. By doing so, you guarantee that all charts are completed. Furthermore, the information pertaining to the patient is fresh in your mind, making it easier to dictate. Make sure that you visit the medical records department once every week or so to check whether more charts need to be dictated or signed. Occasionally, some of your patients may be discharged while you are off. You are still responsible for their charts, however, and should dictate them as soon as you can.

If you receive a warning letter that your privileges could be suspended due to undictated charts, do not delay in completing the charts—just do it. Often, some charts may be listed under your name that are not yours. You must straighten this problem out yourself before your privileges are suspended. Sometimes your dictation may become lost, and you have to repeat it. Maintain a good relationship with the personnel in medical records; they can be of a great help to you.

As mentioned earlier, the discharge summary acts as a link between outpatient and inpatient care. For this reason, it should be adequately detailed, including the cause of admission, any tests performed, all treatments received, any improvements in the patient's condition, items requiring follow-up care on an outpatient basis, and the medication with which the patient was discharged. The most important thing is to indicate a plan for the primary care physician to follow up with the patient. Its inclusion guarantees that the patient will receive the care that was planned during the hospitalization.

KEY POINTS

1. Discharge summaries needed by the hospital for billing purposes and as part of the continuum of patient care.
2. Dictate the minute you discharge the patient.
3. Visit the medical records department once every week or so to check whether more charts need to be dictated or signed.
4. If you receive a warning letter noting that your privileges could be suspended due to undictated charts, do not delay in completing the charts.
5. Discharge summaries act as a link between outpatient and inpatient care.
6. Outline a plan for the primary care physician to follow up with the patient.

SIGN-OUTS

The purpose of sign-outs is to ensure that the continuum of patient care proceeds while you are not in the hospital. If sign-outs are not done properly, they can ruin your career or perhaps injure your patient. To minimize these possibilities, a detailed sign-out to the intern taking over the patient's care is required. Illness is dynamic and can change from one minute to the next. The person to whom you are signing out needs to know the reason for admission, other medical problems, all medications being taken by the patient, any lab work to be checked, and any precautions required with the patient. It can prove frustrating for an intern to be called regarding a patient about whom he or she knows little. Even more frustrating and dangerous is a patient who codes when the on-call intern did not provide a good sign-out. Consequently, you should always make sure that the patient's name, medical record number, location (including room number), active and inactive problems, medication, recent lab work, code status, and things expected to happen and still to do are all listed in an organized fashion before you leave.

If you have an unstable patient, inform the person on call of his or her condition so as to avoid surprises. If something needs to be done for your patient, do it yourself before you leave rather than signing the task out to the on-call intern. The on-call person has many things to do and does not have the time to perform your work as well. Your day should end when your work is done—not when your shift ends. It is important to be courteous by putting yourself in the place of the on-call person and giving him or her the least amount of work possible. Soon it will be your turn to be on call and you will want the same courtesies extended to you.

KEY POINTS

1. Give a detailed sign-out to the intern on call.
2. Include the following items on the sign-out: the patient's name, medical record number, location (including room number), active and inactive problems, medication, recent lab work, code status, and things expected to happen.
3. If you have an unstable patient, inform the person on call of his or her condition to avoid surprises.
4. If something needs to be done for your patient, do it yourself before you leave, rather than signing the task out to the on-call person.

LEARNING AND TEACHING

Some interns and the general public have the misconception that when medical students graduate, they become professionals and cease to be students. Most interns believe that internship and residency provide only practical training and do not require any reading and studying. This fallacy is the biggest trap that awaits you and may prove fatal later in your career. In reality, internship and residency are merely extra years of medical school. They resemble third- and fourth-year medical school, with one exception:

As you advance, you shoulder more responsibilities. Thus you must continue to read and study as long as you are an intern, resident, or attending. Most interns believe that they need only work hard and learn from experiences with patients. You can readily recognize a well-read medical student, intern, resident, or even attending. Reading and studying are ongoing requirements of a physician's life; if you plan to be successful at this profession, they are essential. Learning from your patients is great but never enough. This type of education must be enhanced by book knowledge.

To achieve the best learning and teaching experience, consider the following suggestions. One of the most important principles of any doctor's life can be summarized in this way: You are a student now and always will be one. The more you learn, the better the care that you can give your patient. You have chosen a profession that requires constant reading and updates to keep up with the vast and rapid advances in your field.

Envision the hospital where you are training as another medical school, where everyone around you is a teacher. Try to learn from everyone, including nurses, medical students, physical therapists, respiratory therapists, residents, attendings, other interns, social workers, care coordinators, phlebotomists, physical and occupational therapists, clerks, and most importantly, patients. Every residency program is required to teach you throughout your training. As a consequence, you can ask any question of anyone whom you might reasonably suspect knows the answer. Almost all personnel in the hospital are willing and eager to teach. The only encouragement they require is for you to ask them. If you don't know something, ask. Just because you are a doctor, it doesn't mean that you can't ask a nurse or an aide for help. Everyone is more knowledgeable than you in certain matters. You should not expect only attendings to teach you; others can also impart knowledge to you. You are considered the leader of your team, with the attending physician and the resident acting as your supervisors. For this reason, you must be familiar with all aspects of patient care. Medical school can never prepare you for all of these aspects; instead, they must be learned during your internship.

At the minimum, expect your attending and resident to teach you because it is required. You will come across some attendings and residents who do not try to teach interns, perhaps because they are poor teachers, are just too busy, or are not knowledgeable enough to teach. It is important to be polite and respectful when encouraging them to instruct you. You can accomplish this goal by asking questions during and after rounds. Such inquiries act as both invitations and reminders, and they indicate that you are eager to learn. Another good strategy is to politely ask your attending and resident for guidance. For instance, you might inquire, "Is it possible to discuss this topic before or after rounds?" You might ask the attending and resident to set a specific time every day for teaching rounds.

Another great way to prompt the attending or the resident to teach is to teach yourself. If you read an article the night before, especially one that pertains to your patient, discuss it with the rest of the team on the following day. This practice opens the way for the rest of the team, including the attending, to discuss the topic and encourages them to mention things that were not discussed in the article.

The best way to learn is to teach. If you learn something and teach it to three people within the first 24 hours of learning it, you can almost guarantee that you will retain that information permanently. You can teach it to your resident, attending, nurse, medical student, or co-interns. The ability to teach a topic shows that you understand it.

In particular, even though you are still learning, you have an obligation to teach medical students. Take the time to sit down with them and teach them something you know. Sharing knowledge in this way is part of your duties as a doctor.

You should never be ashamed of not knowing something. After all, medicine is a vast field. No matter how much you think you know, there is always more to learn.

If you are well versed and confident about what you do know, you will not feel ignorant about blanks in your knowledge. Remember that everyone knows his or her own field best, so ask nurses about questions pertaining to their own area of expertise. The same goes for physical therapists, occupational therapists, respiratory therapists, and members of all other disciplines pertaining to patient care.

Noon conferences and the grand rounds are highly valuable experiences. Most interns are so busy that they might never have time to attend any of these events. Some might not even have time to eat lunch. Nevertheless, you should make an effort to attend the noon conferences. They can help you immeasurably, as you will learn critical information. They also offer a chance to change the atmosphere in the middle of the day and take a break. A noon conference is a time to sit with your co-interns and residents, to talk and exchange experiences. It provides time to eat and store the calories needed to keep you going for the rest of the day. Make sure that you make noon conferences a priority—you won't regret it.

You will find reading to be almost impossible at the beginning of your internship. When things settle down, make a routine and stick with it: Learn something every day, no matter what it is or how simple. Every night before retiring to bed, ask yourself this question: What did I learn today? Recall that information. If you can't think of anything, open a book or a journal and read something before nodding off. You will be getting pounds of free journals. Review them and read something pertinent. By reading and learning at least one thing each day, you will feel accomplished.

I developed a good habit when I was a medical student that I have continued to this day. I file every article that I find useful in a cabinet. My files are organized alphabetically according to disease category. I skim through the many journals that I receive, tearing out and saving particularly interesting articles. Keeping journals intact is useless because you might never return to that journal and read all of the articles. Filing pertinent articles by disease category, by contrast, enables you to access them at any time. When I have a patient with a specific disease, I go back to my library and look it up. This approach is a great time saver and has proved very beneficial.

It is extremely important to integrate your medical knowledge with actual patient care. Read regularly, understand what you read, and learn the pathophysiology of each disease rather than just its diagnosis and treatment. You owe it to your patients to understand the physiology of their illnesses and to know everything possible about their diseases and available treatments.

Be observant. Watch everyone around you and see how they do things; use these experiences to learn new skills or to improve existing skills. Observe your resident and attending as they examine your patient; do you do things differently? If you don't know something, don't hesitate to ask your resident or attending. If you are unsure how to do a certain part of the physical exam, ask them. Focus on your weaknesses, and practice and learn until they turn into strengths.

As a doctor, treating patients is only one part of your job. Being a doctor means making a commitment to your patients, your colleagues, and society as whole. You must take care of your colleagues just as you take care of your patients. That is, you must inculcate your fellow caregivers with what you know. It's part of the profession to be both a teacher and a doctor. You have made a commitment to teach everyone, which requires diligence on your part.

The major difference between learning in medical school and learning as part of an internship is that medical school emphasizes memorization so as to pass exams. Unfortunately, most of this knowledge vanishes quickly into the mist. During your internship, you should not try to memorize new information. Your style should change, because no one will test you except when you take your boards (which are not based on memorization). Instead, focus on learning to think and understand. Hone in on the pathophysiology behind each disease and why each symptom or sign develops. Try to apply this pathophysiological information to your patient. This link between book learning and patient care will allow you to remember the information permanently, as it ensures that you under-stand—rather than memorize—knowledge.

"Learning generally occurs when a person asks a question and actively pursues the answer" (1). Ask questions when you attend a lecture. In addition, never turn down an offer to give a lecture—the best way to learn a topic is to speak about it. Along the way, you will discover everything about that subject and retain the knowledge permanently. Read about each problem faced by your patient; this study makes abstract topics become more tangible. Choose a database that you can use for research purposes (such as Medline, Pubmed, or Ovid) during your internship, learn it well, and become proficient at using it.

KEY POINTS

1. An internship and residency are merely added years of medical school; you are a student now and always will be one.
2. Continue to read and study as long as you are an intern, resident, or attending.
3. The more you learn, the better the care that you can give to your patients.
4. Try to learn from everyone around you.
5. If you don't know something, ask someone for help.
6. "Learning generally occurs when a person asks a question and actively pursues the answer" (1).
7. The best way to learn is to teach.
8. If you teach something to three different people within the first 24 hours of learning it, you can almost guarantee that you will retain the information permanently.
9. Expect your attending and resident to teach you because it is required of them.
10. You have an obligation to teach, especially with medical students.
11. Make a vow and stick with it: to learn something every day, no matter what it is or how simple.

12. Use a file cabinet to store and organize articles that you collect.
13. Noon conferences and the grand rounds are highly valuable learning experiences.
14. Integrate your medical knowledge with patient care. Read regularly, understand what you read, and learn the pathophysiology of each disease rather than just its diagnosis and treatment.
15. Be observant, and use your observations to learn new skills or improve existing ones.
16. Learn to think and understand rather than to memorize.

RADIOLOGY ROUNDS

Radiology rounds should be part of your daily routine. They are an integral part of patient care and medical education. Most attendings and residents are too busy to visit the radiology department to check patients' studies. Instead, they tend to rely on the official reports dictated by the radiologist or the documentation of the admitting resident's H&P. Remember that your patient is your responsibility. If you rely on someone else's reading of a film and it turns out to be wrong, resulting in a missed diagnosis, you will be burned just as much as the person who read the film. Furthermore, if you continue to rely on others to read your films, you will never learn how to do it yourself.

Make sure that you go to the radiology department and check your patients' films daily. At the end of rounds, ask the attending physician and the resident to accompany you and review the films jointly. It would help if you called the file room in advance and asked the personnel there to pull out the desired films before you descend on the department (these small courtesies are appreciated by your resident and attending).

If the attending does not have time to look at the films, ask the resident to join you. If the resident doesn't go, go by yourself. Remember that you are doing it for yourself and the patient. If you are not sure how to read a film, ask a radiologist to examine it with you. Don't hesitate to ask the radiologist to teach you about reading the film and anything else that seems unclear to you. It's a good idea to keep a radiology book handy during your internship, as it will be a big help.

KEY POINTS

1. Radiology rounds should be part of your daily routine.
2. At the end of rounds, ask the attending physician and the resident to look at films with you.
3. Call the radiology file room in advance and ask the personnel there to pull out the desired films before you descend on the department.
4. If you are not sure how to read a film, ask a radiologist to examine it with you.
5. It's a good idea to keep a radiology book handy during your internship.

LABORATORY ROUNDS

Most interns never visit the lab to look at peripheral smear, urine, autopsy, hematology, or histology slides. Nevertheless, your education should include visits to various labs in the hospital.

It is a valuable experience to attend the autopsies of your deceased patients, as this activity strengthens your knowledge and understanding of the nature of the disease. If mistakes were made that resulted in a patient's death, you learn a lesson from seeing the cause. It might also bring closure to that case if the cause of death was not known. Seeing with your own eyes is more effective than reading about a topic. It is also a fine way to prepare for taking the boards.

You must understand the pathophysiology of a disease to be able to treat your patient properly. You need to understand all aspects of the illness—including the pathophysiology, molecular biology, and histology—to be able to reach a proper diagnosis and identify an appropriate treatment. Consequently, examining a urine specimen for casts or looking at a peripheral smear may give you a better understanding of the disease.

KEY POINTS

1. Your education should include visits to various labs in the hospital.
2. You must understand the pathophysiology of the disease to be able to treat your patient properly.
3. You must understand all aspects of the illness—including the pathophysiology, molecular biology, and histology—to be able to reach a proper diagnosis and identify an appropriate treatment.

PATIENTS' MEDICATIONS

Most patients who are admitted to a hospital are placed on new medications in addition to the ones they were taking at home. It is important to prescribe the correct medications and, more importantly, to discontinue any unnecessary ones for your patients. Many individuals continue to take superfluous medications for years; they may not understand the whats or whys for their particular drug regimen. Many were placed on certain medications long ago for unknown reasons, and no one bothered to ask whether those drugs were still needed. It is essential that you identify all of your patients' medications and learn why they are necessary.

I once treated a patient who was admitted with multiple sclerosis (MS) exacerbation. In addition to her MS medication, this patient was taking digoxin. When I asked why she was receiving this drug, she stated that she was placed on it many years previously for long-forgotten reasons. I called the primary care physician, who explained that he took over the care of this patient from another physician after he bought the latter doctor's practice. He stated that the patient had been taking digoxin before he assumed responsibility for her care and did not think it was prudent to change it. I called for an EKG and an echocardiogram, which showed a normal sinus rhythm and EF (Ejection fraction) of 60%, respectively. The patient's digoxin level was found to be less than 0.8 ng/mL. At that point, I felt that this medication was unnecessary and should be stopped. When I called the PMD again and informed him of my decision, he agreed with the plan.

Always check the patient's medications upon admission. Some of them might need to be stopped because they could exacerbate the presenting illness. You might not be the admitting person who put the patient on his or her medication, but you will be surprised how many mistakes admitting residents make. For this reason, you should always check someone else's work—even if the other person has far more experience. Most admissions occur late at night, when the admitting resident is apt to be tired and more prone to making errors. Get in the habit of checking all medications taken by the admitted patient and learning why they have been prescribed, even though they may not pertain to the presenting illness. Routinely check patients' medications every day before rounds to ensure that each patient is receiving the appropriate medications.

The best place to confirm patients' daily medications is the nursing medication list. Sometimes an order is written for a medication but not dispensed for some reason. Never assume that just because you prescribed a medication, the patient will receive it automatically—check for yourself.

Make sure that the medication is not contraindicated. Check the patient's kidney and liver function before prescribing certain pharmaceuticals. The drug itself may be prone to causing renal failure or liver failure; be sure to order appropriate tests in such cases. Sometimes patients continue to receive unneeded medication for days or weeks during hospitalization, especially antibiotics. You should always know which day of the antibiotic course the patient is on.

Make sure that you are familiar with all medications administered to your patient while under your care. When the patient is admitted, you immediately become his or her primary caregiver and are responsible for everything taken by the patient. Never leave your patient on any medication unless you know what it is, why it is necessary, and what its most common side effects are. Make sure the patient continues to receive the same medications he or she was taking prior to the hospitalization when applicable.

Most attendings will ask you for the list of your patients' medications; keep this list handy. Occasionally, even the attending physician will not recognize a particular medication; you can demonstrate your knowledge by being familiar with it.

If you have a patient who is acutely ill and a radical change in the lab findings—especially in the patient's liver or kidney function—occurs, immediately suspect the medications to be the culprit. Research them thoroughly.

KEY POINTS

1. Place your patients on the correct medications and, more importantly, do not prescribe any unnecessary drugs.
2. Always check the patient's medications upon admission. Some of them might need to be stopped.
3. Routinely check your patients' medications every day before rounds.
4. The best source of information about patients' medications is the nurses' medication list.
5. Confirm that each patient is actually receiving the prescribed medications daily.
6. Make sure that the medication you prescribe is not contraindicated.
7. Check the patient's kidney and/or liver function before prescribing certain medications.
8. Familiarize yourself with all medications that your patient receives while under your care.
9. If a radical change occurs in the lab findings of an

acutely ill patient, especially changes related to liver or kidney function, immediately suspect the medications to be the culprit.

CONSULT SERVICES

You will be calling for consults throughout your internship. Consultants serve one purpose only: They answer the specific question you asked. They do not become the primary caregivers unless the patient is transferred to their service. You should always run the show and control your patient's care. Try to talk to the resident or attending consultant who sees the patient rather than simply reading the consult form after the fact. A verbal exchange provides the consultant with a fuller picture of the case and helps that person give better recommendations.

You should always understand what was recommended by the consult service. After all, it is part of your patient's care to know what is being recommended and why. If you don't understand something, ask the consultant to explain it to you. Most consultants are eager to teach and would not mind spending a few minutes with you. If they don't have the time or you can't find the answer, ask your resident or attending physician for help or look it up yourself. Your knowledge about your patient's care should be comprehensive.

If the consult service recommends something that does not make sense to you and you believe it's not in the best interest of the patient, don't follow through with it. Run the idea by your resident or attending before accepting it.

For instance, I treated a 450 lb diabetic patient who was admitted with a foot abscess. The X ray of the foot was suspicious of osteomyelitis. An MRI was ordered, and an orthopedic specialist was consulted. The radiology attending physician, upon reading the MRI, confirmed the diagnosis of osteomyelitis. The orthopedic consultant read the chart and wrote a two-line note stating that the orthopedic department would check the X rays and follow up.

Two days later, the consult recommended a bone scan to confirm osteomyelitis, even though the MRI (which is very sensitive for osteomyelitis) had already confirmed this condition. I pointed this fact out to the orthopedic consultant and questioned whether the bone scan was truly necessary. Although the recommendation for the bone scan was not withdrawn, after discussing the matter with the attending physician, we elected not to get this test. The orthopedic consult then recommended that the patient be discharged with instructions to avoid weight bearing on the left foot. This recommendation was impractical: How can you ask a 450 lb man to avoid weight bearing on his foot? Most likely, he would return with his other foot broken after suffering a fall. Therefore, after discussing the situation with my attending physician, we disregarded the orthopedic's recommendation.

Sometimes your patient will be followed by a consult team for the entire duration of his or her hospital stay. Even though consultants may see your patient on a daily basis, you remain the primary caregiver and are responsible for the patient's total care. Always check each consultant's actions and make sure that he or she does not interfere with the rest of the care program. Typically, members of the consult team will focus on only their area of expertise without considering other medical problems.

For instance, I once had a patient who was admitted to our service with acute abdominal pain and found to have small bowel obstruction (SBO). The surgeons were consulted and decided to place a nasogastric tube (NGT) and IVF (intravenous fluids) and keep the patient NPO (nothing per orifice [mouth]). They ran the IVF at 120 cm^3/hour for four days. The patient's pain and abdominal X ray slowly improved. The surgery team saw the patient every morning before 6 A.M. and wrote the same note each day, stating that he was improving and to continue the NGT, NPO, and IVF treatments. On the third day after this regimen was begun, I examined the patient after he was examined by the surgeons. I noted crackles on the bilateral lung fields, and the patient complained of shortness of breath

(SOB). The patient was fluid-overloaded and had baseline coronary artery disease. The calculated input/output (I/O) for the previous three days was found to be −3 L, and a chest X ray showed lung congestion. At this point, the intravenous fluids were stopped and Lasix was administered. When the surgeons visited the patient later that afternoon, they left a note agreeing with the D/C (discontinue) IVF. Later the NGT was discontinued and the SBO resolved. The patient was in more distress and suffered more anxiety from the SOB than he did from the abdominal pain.

What can be learned from this example? Treat the patient as a whole, rather than one symptom at a time.

KEY POINTS

1. Try to talk to the resident or attending consultant who sees the patient rather than reading a consult form after the fact.
2. Make sure that you understand what was recommended by the consult service.
3. Always check on the actions prescribed by consultants and confirm that they do not interfere with the rest of the patient care.
4. Treat the patient as a whole, rather than one symptom at a time.

ANSWERING PAGES

It is very frustrating to page someone and not receive an answer, especially when you don't have time to wait by the phone and the matter is urgent. Be fair to others and answer your pages promptly. Always assume that you are being paged for an important reason (which most often is the case) and respond as soon as possible. What might not be critical to you can be very important to others. Also, the matter might be a simple one that will not take more than a few seconds of your time.

If you don't answer your pages, you might be called via the overhead speaker system or reported to the supervising resident or attending physician. Failure to respond indicates that you are irresponsible, which is not the kind of image you want to present. We all hate pages, but it is something you must learn to live with, if not endure gracefully.

KEY POINTS

1. Answer your pages promptly.
2. Always assume that you are being paged for an important reason.

SICK AND BACK-UP CALLS

When faced with stress and unexpected events, you may sometimes need to call in sick. Most residency programs include a back-up system where people who are on electives cover for those who call in sick. Unfortunately, a few people in each program always take advantage of the system and call in sick often and for unnecessary reasons. If you are tempted to call in sick, keep in mind who will cover for you. Put yourself in that person's shoes and ask how you would feel to be called while you are pursuing your elective. The elective is that time when you work in the field that you enjoy most; it is also a time of light schedules and relief from intense rotations. No one wants to be taken away from this activity. Sooner or later, however, you will work in an elective and be asked to cover for someone else.

Of course, if you are truly ill or a family emergency occurs, you should certainly call in sick. No one will blame you in that situation. Just make sure that you do so only when absolutely necessary.

When you are the designated back-up, keep your pager on at all times. The chief resident can become very testy if you don't respond. The bottom line is to be considerate, do unto others as you would have them do unto you, and maintain good work habits.

If a colleague asks you to cover for him or her and you are able to do so, help out that person. You will be working together for several years, so try to develop a good relationship now and remember that someday you might need the favor returned. It's much easier to ask for help from someone for whom you have covered than from someone whom you refused.

KEY POINTS

1. Keep your pager on at all times.
2. If a colleague asks you to cover for him or her and you are able to do so, help out that person.

REFERENCES

1. Covey SR. The seven habits of highly effective people. New York: Simon and Schuster, 1990.
2. Hurst JW. Thoughts about becoming an intern on a medical service. Resident and Staff Physician 1998;44:69–73.

2

The Surveys

This chapter discusses the results of two surveys. The first survey was randomly given to 50 interns, medical students, residents, nurses, and attendings from various departments (internal medicine, emergency room, surgery, obstetrics and gynecology, family medicine and neurology) at three different institutions (Table 2-1). The second one was given to 50 patients randomly selected from different services (medicine, neurology, family medicine, surgery, and cardiology) at one institution (Table 2-2). The combined surveys were part of a study intended to evaluate postgraduate medical education and its effect on patients' care. They were also used to learn what the various members of the team thought made a good intern (doctor). Respondents were asked to take all the time needed and not use assistance. Instead of choices, they were asked to write what they thought appropriate for each question. Each group surveyed had its own ideas as to what constituted a good intern. The top ten characteristics chosen are shown in Table 2-3. As you will see, there are radical differences in their choices.

FINDINGS BY TYPES OF RESPONDENTS

The degree of personal bias is evident in all groups and is clearly seen as we examine nursing. Fully, 84% of those

---

TABLE 2.1
**The Survey Completed by Nurses, Medical Students,
Interns, Residents, and Attendings**

*Would you please be kind and give your honest opinion about the following
questions:*

Title: attending, PGY1, PGY2, PGY3, nurse, medical student

1. What do you think are the attributes that are necessary to make
   "a good intern"?
2. What do you think are the attributes that might make "a bad
   intern"?

TABLE 2.2
The Survey Completed by Patients

*As you know, you are in a university hospital and you are being cared
for by a team of interns, residents, and attendings. Would you please be
kind and give your honest opinion regarding the following questions:*

1. List the features that you feel are needed to make a "good" intern.
2. List the features that you feel result in a "bad" intern.
3. Are you able to recognize if the doctor taking care of you is an
   attending, a resident, or an intern?
4. Does the system of graduate medical education (an attending
   supervising interns and residents) affect your care? Yes or no
   and how?
5. What things do interns and residents in training need to do, or
   not do, in order to become good future doctors?

---

who responded stated that "Willingness to listen to others, including nurses" is the number one trait a successful intern should have. The reasoning here is obvious: the stereotypical doctor who "knows it all" is a chronic complaint of nurses. Think of the implications for a moment. By simple active listening to the nursing staff you may not only learn something valuable about the patient, but also enhance the self-esteem of the person with whom you are communicating and this solidifies the team. Whether or not you act upon this input should depend on one factor—is the patient's care enhanced?

TABLE 2.3
The Top Ten Attributes That Make "A Good Intern" as Ranked by the Six Groups

Order	Patients	Nurses	Residents	Interns	Attendings	Med. Students
1	Compassion for patients (34, 68%)	Willingness to listen to others, including nurses (42, 84%)	Hard work (26, 52%)	Compassion for patients (23, 46%)	Pleasant, friendly, and humorous personality (22, 44%)	Interest in teaching (25, 50%)
2	Listening to patients (26, 52%)	Compassion for patients (28, 56%)	Team work (19, 38%)	Hard work (21, 42%)	Hard work (18, 36%) Eagerness to learn (18, 36%)	Organization (20, 40%)
3	Ability to explain things to the patient (18, 36%)	Good communication skills (24, 48%)	Compassion for patients (18, 36%) Pleasant, friendly, and humorous personality (18, 36%)	Organization (17, 34%) Good base knowledge (17, 34%)	Compassion for patients (17, 34%)	Compassion for patients (17, 34%)

TABLE 2.3
(continued)

Order	Patients	Nurses	Residents	Interns	Attendings	Med. Students
4	Good knowledge base (13, 26%) Not in a rush (gives patient enough time) (13, 26%)	Respect for others (19, 38%)	Knowing his/her patient well (15, 30%) Good communication skills (15, 30%)	Team work (15, 30%)	Ability to admit when he/she doesn't know (12, 24%) Team work (12, 24%) Well read (12, 24%)	Good communication (15, 30%) Pleasant, friendly, and humorous personality (15, 30%)
5	Good communication skills (11, 22%)	Pleasant, friendly, and humorous personality (17, 34%) Listening to patients (17, 34%)	Eagerness to learn (13, 26%)	Pleasant, friendly, and humorous personality (11, 22%)	Knowing his/her patient well (10, 20%) Respect for others (10, 20%) Good thinking and problem solving skills (10, 20%)	Hard working (14, 28%)

6	Pleasant, friendly, and humorous personality (9, 18%) Humble (9, 18%)	Ability to admit when he/she doesn't know (16, 32%) Eagerness to learn (16, 32%)	Organization (12, 24%)	Good communication skills (10, 20%)	Willingness to listen to others, including nurses (8, 16%) Good communication skills (8, 16%) Takes time for him/herself (exercise, good health, good sleep, good diet, has fun) (8, 16%)	Good base knowledge (13, 26%)
7	Dedication and commitment (7, 14%)	Good knowledge base (15, 30%)	Ability to admit when he/she doesn't know (10, 20%)	Enthusiasm (9, 18%)	Organization (7)	Team work (12, 24%)
8	Ability to follow up on work (6, 12%) Honesty (6, 12%)	Team work (13, 26%) Answering pages promptly (13, 26%)	Responsibility (8, 16%) Good knowledge base (8, 16%)	Efficiency (8, 16%)	Ability to ask for help (6, 12%) Ability to follow up on work (6, 12%)	

TABLE 2.3
(continued)

Order	Patients	Nurses	Residents	Interns	Attendings	Med. Students
	Understanding (6, 12%)				Good knowledge base (6, 12%)	Respect for others (9, 18%)
					Good history taking (6, 12%)	
					Ability to follow instructions (6, 12%)	
9	Respect for others (4, 8%)	Ability to ask for help (10, 20%)	Ability to ask questions (7, 14%)	Respect for others (7, 14%)	Responsibility (5, 10%)	Eagerness to learn (7, 14%)
	Confidence (4, 8%)		Ability to follow up on work (7, 14%)	Honesty (7, 14%)	Common sense (5, 10%)	Efficiency (7, 14%)
	Patience (4, 8%)				Humble (5, 10%)	
					Preparation for rounds (5, 10%)	

10					
Attentiveness (3, 6%)	Humble (8, 16%)	Enthusiasm (6, 12%)	Organization (12, 12%)	Willingness to go beyond (go the extra mile) (5, 10%)	Willingness to listen to others, including nurses (5, 10%)
Good physical examination skills (3, 6%)			Ability to admit when he/she doesn't know (6, 12%)	Thoroughness (5, 10%)	Ability to follow up on work (5, 10%)
Prompt (3, 6%)			Responsibility (6, 12%)	Good procedural skills (4, 8%)	Knowing his/her patient very well (5, 10%)
Professionalism (3, 6%)			Dedication and commitment (6, 12%)	Enthusiasm (4, 8%)	
Team work (3, 6%)				Promptness (4, 8%)	
Willingness to listen to others, including nurses (3, 6%)				Good physical examination skills (4, 8%)	

And what do residents think should be an intern's essential trait? Hard work. As with nursing, residents are looking for interns who are able to simplify their practice. The more industrious the intern, the easier the resident's job becomes. The care of the patient is assured when in the hands of a diligent intern as the resident allows the intern greater autonomy. A lazy and/or a weak intern forces the resident to work harder to ensure the intern is doing his/her job properly, since the resident is responsible for that intern's patients. Furthermore, whatever work the intern leaves behind, the resident has to finish. Overall, a diligent intern provides the patient with the best care because all facets are covered thoroughly and in a timely fashion.

Those interns who were midway through their program chose "compassion for patients" as the attribute that would be most needed to succeed (46%). However, the survey also showed "hard working," "organization," and "team work" in the top four items chosen. It seems that they are in the transition state of moving from "compassion for patients," i.e., personal traits, to the "hard working," i.e., managerial traits as they become residents. They slowly realize the difficulty of their internship and the need to work hard, which in turn takes away from their compassion for their patients. It would be interesting to examine how these priorities might change as they progressed in their internship.

More important than "good knowledge base" (26%), "compassion" was the number one trait (68%) chosen by patients. There are some important implications here. The patient trusts doctors; he assumes that they are qualified until proven otherwise. He does not question their diagnosis or prognosis. What is most important to him is their delivery and their caring attitude. Think of it! The most knowledgeable practitioner with umpteen years of experience and pounds of published items may be considered an "also ran" simply because he lacked or was unable to exhibit compassion.

To attendings, both "hard working" and "eagerness to learn" are very important, but the number one skill they appreciated was "pleasant, friendly, and humorous personality." Why? As the attending supervises the entire team and is ultimately responsible for their choices, he appreciates an intern who not only has good work habits, but is easy to get along with—someone who can take directions easily and with a minimum of fuss. So not only is the perfect intern one who has a relaxed and laid back demeanor, he must also be able to discharge patients quickly and appropriately. As with any other attributes, having a pleasant, friendly, and humorous personality allows patients to open up, trust, and cooperate with their interns. The tension and stress surrounding the patient is relieved by such a doctor dealing with the patient in a friendly manner. It is better and easier to thwart a mean-spirited and unpleasant personality with composure and balance than with an equally obnoxious one.

Not to everyone's surprise, students think that "interest in teaching" should be an intern's distinctive characteristic. Too often the busy intern only hands out scut work for the student to do. Although most students do what they are asked, they would rather have more responsibilities in taking care of the patient. Most students are frustrated by the end of their rotation to work so hard and to learn so little. Their frustration grows further when they hear and see things in front of them without understanding the whys and hows. Interns are extremely busy; they don't have the time to teach medical students or to even learn themselves. However, all they need to do is to talk, talk about their findings or the importance of a particular sign. A medical student is not as capable as an intern and isn't meant to be, but the student who is encouraged may be an extra set of eyes and ears that can help an intern give better patient care. Interns can also show medical students how to instruct so that when they become doctors the cycle continues.

FINDINGS BY TYPE OF TRAIT

Many traits were listed in the overall survey and may be roughly assorted into three categories: personal, managerial, and intellectual. The personal category includes the personal characteristics that one uses to interact with others in their daily life. The managerial qualities are the skills used to do one's job well, more efficiently and in a timely fashion. The intellectual traits include knowledge, learning, applying what's learned, and the ability to think well. Table 2-4 divides all of these traits—including the top ten traits—into those three different categories.

Although there is significant variation among the groups, the personal side of the intern was considered the most important facet (Table 2-4). As discussed, patients held this view close to their hearts. However, there is significant variation among the six groups in choosing this category as number one. Character was most important to patients and nurses (88% and 68%, respectively) and less important to interns and medical students (44.9% and 40.5%, respectively). This category was not the most important for residents and attendings (41.5% and 38.6%, respectively).

In the hierarchy of medical students, interns, residents, and attendings, the emphasis on character declines. Students spend more time with books than with patients, therefore emphasizing the intellectual traits more than personal ones. As students become interns and start working more with patients, their emphasis on personal and managerial traits strengthens while emphasis on intellectual ones declines. Interns have to balance all attributes to please patients, residents, and attendings. As they become residents interns' emphasis on personal attributes declines further; more emphasis is now placed on managerial traits and much less on intellectual ones. This pattern becomes more evident with attendings except that they emphasize intellectual traits more than residents do. This is most likely due to the responsibilities residents and attendings carry managing their patients' care.

"Listening to patients," which is a personal trait, was the number two attribute listed by patients (52%). The only other group that listed this trait among the top ten was nurses (34%). Actually only 8% of the interns, 2% of the attendings, 2% of the medical students, and none of the residents thought it was an important trait. It is possible that those individuals placed more emphasis on the intellectual or the managerial traits. Listening to patients goes against the managerial and the intellectual traits since it takes more time and produces less work.

Managerial attributes are the most important for residents (52%). Residents are more managerial than doctors. They have to manage at least two interns, a few medical students, and the care for patients. They have much less contact with patients and play less of "the doctor role." These attributes become more important to interns. Interns have to manage their patient care and possibly a few students. Although interns interact directly with patients, their main task is to manage the treatment and diagnostic tests recommended by the attending and resident rather than caring for the patient. Managerial traits were also the most important for attendings. Attendings are the executives of the entire team taking care of the patients. These attributes were the least important to patients (8.7%), possibly because they are not aware of the managerial skills required for their care.

The intellectual traits were the least important of all attributes (14.3%). Attendings and medical students thought that these traits are more important (22.5% and 23%, respectively) than the rest of the groups. Medical students are still studying and have to do well on the boards. The higher they score on the boards, the better residency program they qualify for. The current medical education system makes them believe that intelligence is the most important attribute required to become an excellent physician. According to the current system, the better residency program or medical school you attend, the better doctor you are more likely to be and the further you will advance in your career. Attendings still thought that intelligence was an important attribute: that an intelligent intern is able to do his or her job better. Interns and residents come to realize that there is much more to being a doctor than intelligence. Actually residents placed the least emphasis on the intelligence traits (6.5%). They believed that

59

TABLE 2.4
The Top 10 Attributes Divided Into the Three Categories

Group	The Personal (Character) Attributes	The Managerial Attributes	The Intelligence Attributes
Patients	Compassion for patients (34, 68%)	Ability to follow up on work (6, 12%)	Good knowledge base (13, 26%)
	Listening to patients (26, 52%)	Attentiveness (3, 6%)	Good physical examination skills (3, 6%)
	Ability to explain things to the patient (18, 36%)	Prompt (3, 6%)	
	Not in a rush (gives patient enough time) (13, 26%)	Team work (3, 6%)	
	Good communication skills (11, 22%)		
	Pleasant, friendly, and humorous personality (9, 18%)		
	Humble (9, 18%)		
	Dedication and commitment (7, 14%)		
	Honesty (6, 12%)		
	Understanding (6, 12%)		
	Respect for others (4, 8%)		
	Confidence (4, 8%)		
	Patience (4, 8%)		
	Willingness to listen to others, including nurses (3, 6%)		
	Professionalism (3, 6%)		
Nurses	Willingness to listen to others, including nurses (42, 84%)	Team work (13, 26%)	
		Answering pages promptly (13, 26%)	

60

Compassion for patients (28, 56%)
Good communication skills (24, 48%)
Respect for others (19, 38%)
Pleasant, friendly, and humorous personality (17, 34%)
Listening to patients (17, 34%)
Ability to admit when he/she doesn't know (16, 32%)
Ability to ask for help (10, 20%)
Humble (8, 16%)

Eagerness to learn (16, 32%)
Good knowledge base (15, 30%)

Residents

Compassion for patients (18, 36%)
Pleasant, friendly, and humorous personality (18, 36%)
Good communication skills (15, 30%)
Ability to admit when he/she doesn't know (10, 20%)
Ability to ask questions (7, 14%)
Hard work (26, 52%)
Team work (19, 38%)
Knowing his/her patient well (15, 30%)
Organization (12, 24%)
Responsibility (8, 16%)
Ability to follow up on work (7, 14%)

Eagerness to learn (13, 26%)
Good knowledge base (8, 16%)
Enthusiasm (6, 12%)

TABLE 2.4
(continued)

Group	The Personal (Character) Attributes	The Managerial Attributes	The Intelligence Attributes
Interns	Compassion for patients (23, 46%) Pleasant, friendly, and humorous personality (11, 22%) Good communication skills (10, 20%) Enthusiasm (9, 18%) Respect for others (7, 14%) Honesty (7, 14%) Ability to admit when he/she doesn't know (6, 12%) Dedication and commitment (6, 12%)	Hard work (21, 42%) Organization (17, 34%) Team work (15, 30%) Efficiency (8, 16%) Responsibility (6, 12%)	Good base knowledge (17, 34%)
Attendings	Pleasant, friendly, and humorous personality (22, 44%) Compassion for patients (17, 34%) Ability to admit when he/she doesn't know (12, 24%) Respect for others (10, 20%) Willingness to listen to others, including nurses (8, 16%) Good communication skills (8, 16%) Ability to ask for help (6, 12%)	Hard work (18, 36%) Team work (12, 24%) Knowing his/her patient well (10, 20%) Good thinking and problem solving skills (10, 20%) Takes time for him/ herself (exercise, good health, good sleep, good diet, has fun) (8, 16%) Organization (7, 14%) Ability to follow up on work (6, 12%)	

62

	Humble (5, 10%) Enthusiasm (4, 8%)	Ability to follow instructions (6, 12%) Responsibility (5, 10%) Eagerness to learn (18, 36%) Well read (12, 24%) Good knowledge base (6, 12%) Good history taking (6, 12%) Good procedural skills (4, 8%) Good physical examination skills (4, 8%)	Interest in teaching (25, 50%) Good knowledge base (13, 26%) Eagerness to learn (7, 14%) Willingness to listen to others, including nurses (5, 10%) Ability to follow up on work (5, 10%) Knowing his/her patient very well (5, 10%)
Medical Students	Compassion for patients (17, 34%) Good communication skills (15, 30%) Pleasant, friendly, and humorous personality (15, 30%) Respect for others (9, 18%)	Organization (20, 40%) Hard working (14, 28%) Team work (12, 24%) Efficiency (7, 14%)	

63

hard work is more important than intelligence to make a better intern.

Overall, the personal traits were considered more important than the other two. This is surprising since most acceptances to medical schools and residency programs are based on MCAT and board scores, supposedly a measure of intelligence. It's true that while those programs interview the candidates to see whether or not they are likable, more emphasis is placed on scores and intelligence rather than on character. Meeting someone for 10 or 20 minutes in an interview, or reading a recommendation letter written on his or her behalf does not tell much about that person's character. Furthermore, the questions asked during an interview are so superficial and predictable that most candidates are well prepared to answer them. There should be a more intensive and standardized method of assessing character. The survey shows that character is the most important criterion required to make a good doctor. There are many students that graduate from Ivy League schools with excellent scores who fail to interact well with patients because of the lack of character skills. Does this make them good doctors? Maybe they just need training to integrate intelligence with good character. Intelligence is useless unless it is properly transformed into practical care for patients.

The managerial characteristics seem to be even more important than the intellectual ones. How many medical schools or residency programs do you know that teach their students those skills? No one asks in an interview about managerial skills. Modern medicine is much different from the old fashioned one where doctors treated patients and never worried about a system controlled by insurance companies, legal stains, and many other obstacles. With the emerging health care system, there is much more to being a good doctor than caring for the patient. Currently, medicine is more of a business—ranging from large (hospitals) to small (private practices). Many management skills are needed to be able to run this business properly. If we can't go back to a more traditional medicine, which is not a practical choice, we can learn more about the "business of doctoring" and hopefully be better able to balance between them.

SUMMARY

Although the survey is limited, it still points out some of the criteria that might be used by interns to become better doctors. One of the surveys' limitations is the number of individuals polled. The surveys did not provide choices that individuals were able to choose from; they used a free-style format. This was done to allow individuals to choose what they thought was important without being influenced by suggestions. It is interesting that only 40% of the patients surveyed were able to distinguish between interns and attendings—creating a crossover effect for both groups (Table 2-5). Only 20% of patients felt the system of graduate medical education affected their care (Table 2-6).

KEY POINTS

1. The survey was completed by 50 patients, nurses, attendings, medical students, residents, and interns (total of 300 individuals).
2. The degree of personal bias is evident in all groups.
3. 84% of nurses stated that "Willingness to listen to others, including nurses" is the number one trait a successful intern should have.

TABLE 2.5 Patients' Responses to the Question: Are You Able to Recognize if the Doctor Taking Care of You Is an Attending, a Resident, or an Intern?	
Yes	20 (40%)
No	25 (50%)
Sometimes	5 (10%)
Total	50 (100%)

TABLE 2.6
Patients' Responses to the Question: Does the System of Graduate Medical Education (an Attending Supervising Interns and Residents) Affect Your Care? Yes or No and How?

Yes	20 (40%)	Good Effect: 16 (80%)
		Bad Effect: 4 (20%)
No	21 (42%)	
Unsure	3 (6%)	
No answer	6 (12%)	
Total	50 (100%)	

4. Residents think hard work is the number one trait.

5. Those interns who were midway through their program chose "compassion for patients" as the attribute that would be most needed to succeed (46%).

6. More important than "good knowledge base" (26%), "compassion" was the number one trait (68%) chosen by patients.

7. To attendings, both "hard working" and "eagerness to learn" are very important, but the number one skill they appreciated was "pleasant, friendly, and humorous personality."

8. Students think that "interest in teaching" should be an intern's distinctive characteristic.

9. The various traits listed in the survey may be roughly assorted into three categories: personal, managerial, and intellectual (Table 2-4).

10. The personal side of the intern was considered the most important facet.

11. In the upward hierarchy of medical students, interns, residents, and attendings, the emphasis on character declines.

12. Managerial attributes are the most important for residents (52%).

13. The intellectual traits were the least important of all attributes (14.3%).

3

Evidence-Based Medicine

Evidence-based medicine (EBM) is a new paradigm in the practice of medicine that has emerged in the past few years due to new developments in clinical research. It has led to more effective use of medical literature in guiding the physician. In EBM, clinical experience, good clinical skills, clinical instinct, and sensitivity to patients' emotional needs are all necessary in becoming a competent physician (6). This paradigm also suggests that understanding the basic mechanisms of the disease under scrutiny and its patho-physiology is necessary, but insufficient to ensure good clinical practice (6).

EBM requires physicians to learn new skills, including ways to efficiently research clinical literature and the appli-cation of particular rules in evaluating that literature. To apply EBM, physicians must follow five steps (12):

1. Precisely identify the problem and the information needed to resolve it. (13)
2. Conduct a comprehensive literature search that locates several articles addressing the problem. (13)
3. Select the best and most relevant article relating to your patient. (13)
4. Validate this literature to see whether it applies to your patient. (13)

5. Understand the article and be able to present and discuss it with colleagues to resolve the problem. (6)

STEP 1: IDENTIFY THE PROBLEM AND INFORMATION NEEDED TO RESOLVE IT

The first step in EBM is to formulate a question that addresses your patient's problem. This question can be classified into one of four categories: diagnostic tests, treatments, prognosis, or general review (6). It should be precise and clear, and it should deal with a specific issue that relates to the patient. It is important to develop a thorough mental picture of your needs so as to remain focused, particularly if you are reviewing multiple sources (2).

For instance, to study the effectiveness of spironolactone (aldactone) on a patient with congestive heart failure (CHF), you might formulate the following question: Does aldactone reduce mortality in patients with moderate to severe CHF? To decide between using heparin or lovenox for unstable angina, you might ask a different question: which anticoagulant agent—heparin or enoxaparin (lovenox) is more effective in treating patients with unstable angina? To find out whether you should initiate Coumadin therapy with 5 mg or 10 mg in your patient, ask this question: Is it better to initiate Coumadin therapy with a 5 mg or a 10 mg dose? (12) To discover whether prophylactic oophorectomy might be helpful in preventing ovarian cancer in a patient who has a family history of the disease, formulate the following question: Does prophylactic oophorectomy prevent ovarian cancer in women with a family history of ovarian cancer? All of the preceding questions are precise and deal with either treatment, diagnosis, or prognosis.

STEP 2: CONDUCT A COMPREHENSIVE LITERATURE SEARCH

The second step in EBM is to find a source that might answer your question. The first and easiest route is to ask one of your colleagues or a consultant who specializes in the relevant field. If your source is not completely sure about the answer or you receive different responses from different colleagues, you may prefer to seek out a different source to answer your question. This strategy is, however, only effective when the question concerns an exposure, treatment, or patient you are unlikely to see again (11). If the question deals with basic pathophysiology or general information, a textbook is a good source. In particular, *Harrison's Principles of Internal Medicine* (1), *Cecil Textbook of Medicine* (3), and *Kelly's Textbook of Internal Medicine* (9) are all good references.

If you are looking up the latest information about a certain drug, the MEDLINE database has limited value, because a time lag separates the publication of an article and its indexing in the database (2). A better place to search for drug-related information is Drug Facts & Comparison. This database is updated monthly with interactions and prescribing information. Most hospitals also have their own databases, which are generally up-to-date and readily accessible (2).

To answer questions pertaining to prognosis, diagnosis, and treatment, it is important to find a reliable database. Greatful Med is an excellent choice in such cases. Published clinical guidelines represent another good source (11); they are based on selected articles that were published in the past and are reviewed and agreed upon by several specialists in that field. Best Evidence and the Cochrane Library are also excellent sources to use. You can also look for relevant articles in your own library, as recommended in Chapter 1.

If you are unfamiliar with use of these computer databases, go to the library and ask for guidance. Choose a database with which you feel comfortable, then learn it and stick with it. Don't jump from one database to another.

STEP 3: SELECT THE MOST RELEVANT ARTICLE

The third step of EBM is to select the best and most relevant article that might answer your question. Your search should yield several possibilities, depending on the keywords used. Survey the titles and choose the ones that appear to be directly relevant to your question or answer it most accurately (13). Narrow the field down to one article that you believe best answers your question.

STEP 4: VALIDATE THE LITERATURE AS APPLYING TO YOUR PATIENT

Now that you have the article, the fourth step is to validate and critically appraise its quality of evidence and its applicability to your patient. This phase entails identifying the nature of the article and the type of study that it describes. Four general types of studies exist: those that address questions pertaining to treatment, prognosis, etiology or causation, and diagnosis (13). Make sure that the article meets the criteria for valid investigation on that particular topic. In addition, ensure that the results are applicable to your patient (13).

For example, if your question addresses a diagnostic test, you might validate the article by asking the following questions (4):

- Was the appropriate diagnostic test used to diagnose the disease?
- Were the correct spectrum of patient samples (mild and severe, treated and untreated disease) used in the study?
- Was there an independent blind comparison of the diagnosis?

If your question addresses a treatment issue, you might validate the article by asking these questions:

- Were the treatments randomized? (5)
- Do the authors account for all patients entered in the study? (5)

- Are the study results valid and will they help you care for your patient? (8)

If your question deals with a review article, you might ask the following:

- Were definitive methods used to decide which articles to include in the review? (10)

The strongest evidence in guiding treatment decisions is best taken from randomized studies. Such trials should report all relevant clinical outcomes, as well as morbidity and mortality data and data on subjects who dropped out or who didn't conform to the intended treatment (13). In all cases, you should ask these additional questions (13):

- Are the study patients similar to my patient? (If the answer to this question is "no," then even statistically significant results will not be applicable to your patient.)
- Is the clinical significance of the outcomes addressed?
- Is the treatment feasible?

Furthermore, the recommended intervention must be "available, affordable, and acceptable to the patient." The recommended therapy must also be important enough to justify the interventions (13).

STEP 5: UNDERSTAND THE ARTICLE THOROUGHLY

The fifth step in EBM is to understand the article and be able to present and discuss it with your colleagues as you seek to answer your question (6). Read the article scrupulously, from the methods used to the conclusion. Understanding the article and being able to present it guarantees that you will remember it and be able to extend your new knowledge to later patients. Remember that you are not doing this research for a test; you are doing it to help both your current patient and subsequent patients.

APPLICATION OF EBM IN CLINICAL PRACTICE

One way to apply EBM is to suggest to your attending physician or resident that it be incorporated into clinical team rounds. Although the process of searching for and studying relevant articles might be time-consuming, it has proved to be beneficial. House staff members believe that more than 90% of the searches that are stimulated by patient problems lead to some improvement in patient care (14).

Sackett and Straus (14) investigated this issue by incorporating an "evidence cart" into clinical rounds. This cart contained Critically Appraised Topics (CATs), Redbook (developed by Nuffield Department of Medicine), Best Evidence, JAMA Rational Clinical Examination series, The Cochrane Library, MEDLINE, a physical examination textbook, a radiology anatomy textbook, and a Simulscope that allowed several people to listen simultaneously to the same signs on physical examination. In the study, 79 of 98 searches (81%) sought evidence that could affect diagnostic and treatment decisions. In addition, 71 of those 79 searches (90%) regarding patient management were successful. Of the 71 successful searches, 52% confirmed the current or provisional diagnostic or treatment plan; 25% led to selection of a new diagnostic skill, additional test, or new management decision; and 23% corrected a previous clinical skill, diagnostic test, or treatment. The only problem that the group participating in the study encountered was an inability to take the cart to the bedside due to its bulkiness.

Today, multiple textbooks and references can be placed on one CD-ROM and easily carried. A laptop computer can be toted on rounds with little effort, and multiple searches can be performed at the patient's bedside. The laptop can be connected to the Internet at many nursing stations and searches subsequently performed. Adapting to this way of teaching makes rounds and patient care much more effective. Consider mentioning it to your attending at the beginning of your internship rotation.

KEY POINTS

1. Evidence-based medicine (EBM) is a new paradigm in the practice of medicine that has emerged due to on-going developments in clinical research.

2. EBM leads to more effective use of medical literature in guiding the physician in caring for patients.

3. In EBM, clinical experience, good skills, clinical instincts, and sensitivity to patients' emotional needs are all considered important to becoming a competent physician.

4. EBM requires physicians to gain new skills, including the ability to efficiently research clinical literature and to apply particular rules in evaluating the articles identified in this manner.

5. The first step in EBM is to precisely identify the problem and the information needed to resolve it.

6. Your question can be classified into one of four categories: diagnostic tests, treatments, prognosis, or general review.

7. The second step in EBM is to conduct a comprehensive literature search that locates several articles addressing the problem.

8. The third step in EBM is to select the best and most relevant article pertaining to your case.

9. The fourth step in EBM is to validate the literature to confirm that it applies to your patient.

10. The fifth step in EBM is to understand the article and be able to present it to and discuss it with colleagues so as to resolve the problem.

11. If you are searching for the latest information about a drug, the Drug Facts & Comparison database is a good source.

12. If you are answering a question pertaining to prognosis, diagnosis, or treatment, Greatful Med is a reliable database.

13. If you want to know about basic pathophysiology or general information, a textbook is a good source.

REFERENCES

1. Braunwald E, Fauci AS, Kasper DL, Hauser SL, Longo DL, and Jamson JL. Harrison's Principles of Internal Medicine, 15th ed. New York: McGraw-Hill, 2001.
2. Brennan DP. Bibliographic database searching: Finding the right information. St. Francis Journal of Medicine 1997; 3(3): 122–125.
3. Cecil RL, Bennett JC and Goldman L. Cecil Textbook of Medicine, 21st ed. Philadelphia: Saunders Company, 2000.
4. Department of Clinical Epidemiology and Biostatistics, McMaster University. How to read clinical journals, II: to learn about a diagnostic test. Can Med Assoc J 1981;124:703–710.
5. Department of Clinical Epidemiology and Biostatistics, McMaster University. How to read clinical journals, V: to distinguish useful from useless or even harmful therapy. Can Med Assoc J 1981;124:1156–1162.
6. Evidence-Based Medicine Working Group. Evidence-Based Medicine: a new approach to teaching the practice of medicine. JAMA, November 4, 1992; 268:2420–2425.
7. Guyatt GH, Sackett DL and Cook DJ. Users' Guides to the Medical Literature. II. How to use an article about therapy or prevention. B. What were the results and will they help me in caring for my patients? JAMA, January 1994; 271 (1): 59–63.
8. Guyatt GH, Sackett DL and Cook DJ. Users' Guides to the Medical Literature. II. How to use an article about therapy or prevention. A. Are the results of the study valid? JAMA, December 1993; 270 (21): 2598–2601.
9. Kelley WN. The Textbook of Internal Medicine, 4th ed. Philadelphia: Lippincott-Raven, 2000.
10. Oxman AD, Guyatt GH. Guidelines for reading literature reviews. Can Med Assoc J 1988;138:697–703.
11. Oxman AD, Sackett DL, Guyatt GH. Users' guides to the medical literature: I. How to get started. JAMA 1993;270: 2093–2095.
12. POEMs: patient oriented evidence that matters. J Family Practice 1999;48:247–254.
13. Sackett DL, Haynes RB, Guyatt GH, Tugwell P. Clinical epidemiology: a basic science for clinical medicine, 2nd ed. Boston: Little, Brown, 1991:173–186.
14. Sackett DL and Straus. Finding and applying evidence during clinical rounds: The "Evidence Cart". JAMA 1998; 280(15): 1336–1338.

4

The On-Call Time

The "on-call" time is the least favorite period for most interns. Despite its burdens, this time is also the most valuable because you can enjoy some independence. It's a time when your experience and judgment come to the fore. If you prepare for your call wisely, you will enjoy it and make the most of it.

This chapter provides some tips that might make your call less onerous. First, start your call with a positive attitude. Arriving with a negative attitude will not get you out of the job; instead, your distaste will merely make things worse. If you approach the work enthusiastically, things will go more smoothly and you might even enjoy yourself. How do you achieve a positive attitude toward doing a call? Think of it as a time to see and do new things. You will learn how to be independent and function under pressure. Night calls can be quiet, because the atmosphere tends to be more subdued.

It is important to take a professional approach and arrive on time or even a few minutes early. If you are starting your call immediately after your shift ends, obtain a detailed sign-out from the other interns in a timely fashion. Know which patients are unstable and learn their code status. Know why they are unstable and what to do in case something goes wrong. Find out what you need to check for every patient.

After sign-out, visit the stations and say "hello" to the nurses. Make them aware that you are on call and give them your beeper number. This time is when being considerate to nurses pays off. Ask whether anything must be ordered or renewed. By taking this step at the beginning of the night, you may dramatically reduce the number of pages later during the on-call time.

Check the sign-out list and finish any incomplete items on it. Now, you can go to your room to relax, do some reading, or sleep. Around 11:30 P.M. or after the change of the nursing shift, return to each nursing station and ask whether anything needs to be done. Night nurses are a different breed, so take the time to simply talk with them. The change of shift is a time when new orders arise, as the nurses are signing out to one another. After completing any unfinished tasks, you can go to your room and get some sleep. Try to sleep every minute you can.

Of course, you must still answer your pages at all times. If working with one or two nursing stations, give your phone number to the call room, indicating where you can be found. You can then be called directly, which is preferable because you won't have to dial in every time. Some people hear the phone better than the pager. More importantly, you can assure yourself that you won't sleep through a page, as the nurse will call until you answer. Some interns prefer staying up instead of sleeping; others sleep any chance they get after midnight. Sometimes you can get lucky and not be called for hours. The more sleep you get, the more normal your life will be.

When a code is called, you should be the first person to respond. You will be the one that other personnel running the code look to for pertinent information. Now is when you can do central lines, arterial sticks, and intubation. Be aggressive during the code. No one, including your resident, will ask whether you want to do a central line. You must ask for permission to place it, perform an arterial stick, or intubate the patient. Keep your eyes and ears open during the code and observe everything around you. Recall those ACLS (advanced cardiac life support) skills that you read about but may have since forgotten. Keep in mind that next year you will be running the code. Always know what's being done and why, because you must document the code when it's finished.

Document all major events with a date and time. These data are recorded for two reasons: for legal purposes and to help the morning team know what happened overnight. Make sure that the documentation is detailed enough to explain the reason for the call, your diagnosis or line of thinking, the management recommended, and items that require follow-up.

In the morning, sign out all important occurrences even though you documented them in the chart. Be courteous and be at the place of sign-out on time. The morning team members need to start their day early to take care of their patients. Remember—the earlier you sign out, the earlier you go home.

When you go home, try to sleep immediately, so that you can enjoy the rest of the day. It's better to sleep when possible during the call and take a short nap during the day. Some individuals will not sleep during the call, then go home and crash. This routine can prove numbing for those who are doing at least two weeks of night float. Those two weeks will be lost in a fog. It is better to sleep a little when possible, take a nap during the day, and have a few hours for yourself.

5

On-Call Common Problems

This chapter offers guidelines for handling the common problems faced by an intern during a call. It is essential to keep in mind that these suggestions are merely general guidelines, providing quick hints on how to approach these calls. They are certainly not comprehensive enough to treat these conditions. If you are not sure how to deal with a particular call, consult a comprehensive reference for additional details. In any case, you must see the patient, examine him or her, and identify all essential information before ordering any test or other action. Keep in mind that the history taking and physical exam provide 85% of the information needed for patient diagnosis.

Consider an incident that happened to an intern at a major teaching institute while on call. The intern was summoned to see a patient who was tachycardiac while undergoing telemetry to rule out myocardial infarction (MI). A 12-lead EKG showed supraventricular tachycardia (SVT). The intern focused on the patient's heart rate, assuming that this problem occurred secondary to MI. She gave the patient Cardizem IV, repeating the dose several times. After receiving three doses, the patient became hypotensive and coded, then was transferred to the intensive care unit. An examination of the patient revealed that he had a rigid and severely tender abdomen, which later proved to be a perforated ulcer; he died that night. In this case, the intern failed to examine the patient and administered a drug that exacerbated his hypotension. The lesson from this example is clear: Always examine the patient before prescribing any medication and do not focus on the obvious.

Following are some general guidelines that you should follow for each call:

1. Get as much detailed information as possible from the nurse.
2. Obtain the vital signs on each patient.
3. Ask the nurse for the reason of admission on each patient.
4. Take a good history and perform a physical exam of the patient if necessary.
5. If the call is urgent, do not delay.

ABDOMINAL PAIN

1. Did the patient have any recent surgeries? Is the patient passing flatus? When was his or her last bowel movement? Flatus is a good sign to rule out bowel obstruction.
2. Distinguish between an acute abdomen and a non-urgent one.
3. Even mild abdominal pain in patients who are taking steroids is significant. Steroids can mask the severity of the abdominal pain and the fever.
4. Many calls for abdominal pain occur secondary to constipation. The patient may note that he or she has not experienced a bowel movement for days. If so, you can give either an enema or *Lactulose or milk of magnesia 30 cc PO Q4h until the first bowel movement occurs.*
5. If abdominal distention is present without localized

pain, order a STAT flat and upright abdominal x-ray to rule out obstruction.

6. If you suspect acute surgical abdomen (including perforated or ruptured viscus, ruptured intra-abdominal abscess, intra-abdominal hemorrhage, or viscous necrosis), keep the patient NPO and call your resident and a STAT surgery consult.

7. If you suspect peptic ulcer disease or gastroesophageal reflux disease (GERD), give *aluminum and magnesium hydroxide (Maalox) 30 cc PO × 1* and start an H_2 blocker *(famotidine [Pepcid] 20 mg PO BID)* or proton pump inhibitor *(omeprazole [Prilosec] 20 mg PO QD, or pantoprazole [Protonix] 40 mg PO QD).* You can use other H_2 blockers or proton pump inhibitors.

8. Consider the following etiologies, all of which may be associated with abdominal pain:
   - *Fever:* Consider intra-abdominal infection or inflammation.
   - *Hypotension:* Consider gastrointestinal (GI) bleeding (see "GI Bleeding") or septic shock.
   - *Brown feculent emesis:* Consider bowel obstruction.
   - *Frank blood:* This finding is suggestive of upper GI bleeding.
   - *Diarrhea:* Acute pancreatitis, an infectious source, or a small bowel obstruction or ischemic bowel disease.
   - *A history of alcohol abuse:* Consider spontaneous bacterial peritonitis.
   - *A history of coronary artery disease (CAD):* Consider ischemic bowel disease.
   - *A previous abdominal surgery:* Consider adhesions.
   - *The patient is on anticoagulation therapy:* Consider intra-abdominal hemorrhage.

9. Consider the type of abdominal pain:
   - Burning: peptic ulcer.
   - Sudden constant and severe, perhaps radiating to the shoulder or neck: perforated ulcer.
   - Sharp and constricting pain that perhaps radiating to the inferior angle of the right scapula: biliary colic.

- Deep agonizing, radiating to the back: acute pancreatitis.
- Gripping with intermittent worsening: bowel obstruction.

AGITATION

1. Check whether any of the patient's medications might cause withdrawal symptoms.
2. Inquire about the patient's history of alcohol use to rule out alcohol withdrawal.
3. Some patients might be frustrated with being in the hospital or their illness and might just need to talk to someone and be reassured that they will recover.
4. Rule out any central nervous system (CNS) or metabolic disorder that might cause agitation by taking a good history, examining the patient, checking his or her medications, and ordering any necessary lab tests—serum chemistry, CBC (complete blood count) with differential, PT/APTT (prothrombin time/activated partial thromboplastin time), liver panel, TSH (thyroid stimulating hormone) ammonia levels, and/or anion gap.
5. If the patient is extremely agitated (for example, trying to remove the IV line or climbing out of bed) and the medication did not work, you might need to restrain the patient's wrists or ankles, or use a "posey."
6. If the patient shows any threat to himself or herself or to other people, you might need to place him or her on one-to-one observation.
7. In older patients, a good medication to give is *haloperidol (Haldol) 1–5 mg IM × 1*. You may repeat this medication at *1–3 mg PO* until the patient's agitation is controlled. Watch for hypotension and dystonia, both of which are common side effects with the drug. If hypotension develops, you can give intravenous fluids. If dystonia develops, you can give *diphenhydramine (Benadryl) 25–50 mg PO, IM, IV × 1.* Older patients

with baseline dementia can also have intensive care unit (ICU) psychosis and sundown phenomenon. Haldol is a good choice for those patients (starting with the smallest dose possible and going up). In younger patients, you can use *lorazepam (Ativan) 1–3 mg IV or 5 mg PO × 1.*

8. Another choice instead of Haldol is *chlorpromazine (Thorazine) 25–50 mg PO or IM Q3–4h.*

9. If you suspect that the agitation is due to anxiety, *alprazolam (Xanax) 0.25–0.5 mg PO Q8 PRN* is a good choice.

10. If you are in the critical care unit (CCU) or ICU and the patient is intubated, you might use *midazolam (Versed) with a loading dose of 0.2–0.35 mg/kg IV over 20–30 seconds,* then keep the patient on the appropriate drip to maintain sedation. Versed has the advantage of causing amnesia.

ARRHYTHMIAS

1. Arrhythmias are serious. You need to examine the patient immediately and take a detailed history.

2. Get an idea from the nurse as to what type of arrhythmia the patient is having—fast, slow, or irregular. This information will help you determine the urgency of the matter.

3. Determine whether the patient is symptomatic (especially chest pain, SOB, and lightheadedness).

4. Ask the nurse to perform a 12-lead EKG, then go see the patient.

5. If the patient has an arrhythmia with symptoms, call your resident.

6. Most patients with arrhythmia require oxygen. Start with N/C (nasal canula) at 2 L.

The remainder of this section discusses some common arrhythmias that you might encounter during your call.

Atrial Fibrillation

1. If the patient is unstable (that is, hypotensive, chest pain or SOB) and the episode is acute, you need to perform cardioversion beginning with 100 J.
2. If the patient is stable, you can give *diltiazem (Cardizem) 20 mg IV × 1*. If no response occurs, repeat with *25 mg IVP*. Another option is to give *metoprolol (Lopressor) 5 mg IVP*. If the patient develops hypotension after administration of these medications, you can always give IVF—but be careful with CHF patients. You can also load the patient with *digoxin (Lanoxin) 0.25 mg IV or PO Q4h × 4* doses, then *0.125–0.5 mg PO QD*.

None of the drugs mentioned here will convert the patient into sinus rhythm; they merely control the heart rate. As long as the rate is controlled, you don't need to worry about the rhythm during your call, unless the patient is unstable. Also, digoxin is not used to control the rate immediately. It takes some time to kick in, so you initially need to control the rate with a different medication.

Atrial Flutter

Treat this condition in the same way as atrial fibrillation.

Multifocal Atrial Tachycardia

1. Look for a cause.
2. Alternatively, start *verapamil (Calan) 80 mg PO Q8h* or *diltiazem (Cardizem) 30 mg PO Q6h* (for rate control).

Sinus Tachycardia with PACs (Premature Atrial Contractions)

No urgent treatment needed. If necessary, however, you can treat this condition in the same way as multifocal atrial tachycardia.

Sinus Tachycardia with PVCs (Premature Ventricular Contractions)

Common causes of PVCs include myocardial ischemia, cardiomyopathy, mitral valve prolapse, hyperthyroidism, hypoxia, hypokalemia, and digoxin toxicity. During your call, you need to be concerned with couplet PVCs (more than three). If the patient is having more than five PVCs, it is considered nonsustained ventricular tachycardia (VT), which you might need to treat.

Sinus Tachycardia

Causes of this condition include fever, hypotension, hypoxia, anxiety, pain, hyperthyroidism, and use of certain medications. Treat the cause.

Supraventricular Tachycardia (SVT)

1. If the SVT patient is unstable (hypotensive, chest pain or SOB), perform synchronized cardioversion, starting at 100 J.
2. If the patient is stable, perform the *valsalva maneuver* (ask the patient to hold his or her breath or bear down as if having a bowel movement). You can also do *carotid sinus massage* (only if the patient is on continuous EKG monitoring and with atropine available). If all else fails, give *adenosine 6 mg IV bolus; repeat a second time with 12 mg; and give a third time with 18 mg IV push.* You can also give *diltiazem (Cardizem) 20 mg IVP.* Repeat with *25 mg IVP.* You can use *verapamil (Calan) 2.5 mg IV over 2 minutes; repeat every 5–10 minutes.* **Do not** give verapamil if you suspect wide complex tachycardia.

Ventricular Tachycardia (VT)

VT is commonly associated with hypotension. If the patient is unstable (no pulse or blood pressure), call a code and proceed. You need to get a *12- lead EKG*, place the patient on *100% O₂ mask*, and give *lidocaine 1 mg/kg bolus.* You can repeat the same dose in 5–15 minutes. If lidocaine is ineffective, give *procainamide 100 mg IV given at a rate of 50 mg/min up to 1000mg, followed by an infusion of 20-80 μg/kg/min*. You can also do *cardioversion beginning at 100 J*.

Ventricular Fibrillation

Call a code and follow the ACLS algorithm.

Sinus Bradycardia

1. Make sure the patient is not on any beta blockers, calcium-channel blockers, or digoxin.
2. For a heart rate of less than 40/min, give *atropine 0.5 mg IV push*. If no response occurs, repeat every 5 minutes until reaching the maximum dose of 2 mg IV.
3. If no response occurs, you may use *isoproterenol (Isuprel) infusion by adding 2 mg of isoproterenol to 500 mL D5W running at 1–10 μg/min (15–150 mL/h)*.

CHANGE IN MENTAL STATUS

1. Ask the nurse to clarify the change in mental status (as confusion, agitation, drowsiness, stupor, or coma).
2. If the patient is diabetic, ask the nurse to get a STAT finger stick.
3. If the patient is experiencing chest pain or shortness of breath, order pulse oximetry. If it is low, get a STAT ABG (arterial blood gas) and place the patient on O_2. Start with 2 L N/C.
4. Ask whether the patient sustained any recent trauma.
5. Ask whether the patient has a history of alcohol use. If so, when was his or her last drink? If you suspect alcohol withdrawal, follow the recommendations for management of alcohol withdrawal.

Common conditions that might result in a change in mental status include the following:

1. *Hypertension:* causes hypertensive encephalopathy.
2. *Fever:* suggestive of delirium tremens (DT), sepsis, or cerebral vasculitis.
3. *Tachycardia:* suggestive of sepsis, hyperthyroidism, DT, or hypoglycemia.
4. *Diabetes:* results in hypoglycemia or hyperglycemia. Get STAT finger stick and treat accordingly.
5. *Tachypnea:* suggestive of hypoxia. Auscultate the lungs and order pulse oximetry; if it is low, get a STAT ABG and place the patient on O_2 (2 L N/C and adjust as necessary).
6. *Nuchal rigidity and/or a headache:* suggestive of meningitis or subarachnoid hemorrhage. Get a STAT computed tomography (CT) scan of the head, call your resident, and consider a lumbar puncture.
7. *Focal neurological deficits:* suggestive of a stroke. Get a STAT CT scan, call your resident, and ask for a STAT neurology consult. If the patient is diabetic, get a finger stick. Hypoglycemia can produce focal neurological deficits.
8. *History of alcohol abuse*: suggestive of alcohol withdrawal. Other symptoms you might see in these patients include fever, tremor, visual hallucinations, tachycardia, dilated pupils, and diaphoresis. It manifests within 24–72 hours after the last alcoholic drink. Treat urgently. Load the patient with *diazepam (Valium) 5–10 mg IV Q 30 minutes until patient is sedated;* then prescribe a maintenance dose of *10–20 mg PO Q6h.* You can also use *chlordiazepoxide (Librium) 25–100 mg PO Q6h for several days*. The dose may be tapered later. Also give *thiamine 100 mg IV QD for five days and folic acid 1 mg PO QD.* If the patient is not in DT but you suspect it, give the following:
   - *Chlordiazepoxide (Librium): 50 mg PO Q3–4h PRN; maximum dose of 300 mg/day*
   - *Diphenhydramine (Benadryl): 50 mg PO Q HS PRN for 3 days*
   - *Thiamine: 100 mg PO QD*
   - *Multivitamins: 1 tab PO QD*

- *Folic acid: 1 mg PO QD*
- *Tylenol: 650 mg PO Q4h PRN for headache or muscle pain*

9. *Medications*: one of the most common causes of change in mental status. Determine whether the patient recently began any new medications and look up their side effects.
10. *Postoperative patients*: A change in mental status can be a side effect of analgesics, anesthetics, or fluids and electrolyte imbalance.

CHEST PAIN

Chest pain is an urgent call with which you have to deal immediately.

1. Differential diagnosis for chest pain:
   - *Myocardial ischemia:* substernal crushing/pressure-like pain, radiating to the jaw, neck, and left arm. The pain can be associated with SOB, nausea, diaphoresis, lightheadedness, and/or numbness of the left arm (especially the medial aspect). Myocardial ischemia can present in many ways. In diabetics, it may appear as a substernal burning sensation, epigastric pain, or silently without pain.
   - *Aortic dissection:* severe tearing or ripping pain radiating to the back.
   - *Pneumonia, pulmonary embolism, pericarditis, costocondritis:* pleuritic chest pain.
   - *Costocondritis:* reproducible pain with palpation around the sternal border without radiation.
   - *GERD*: can commonly mimic myocardial chest pain.
2. Get a 12-lead EKG.
3. Get details from that patient about the type of chest pain and do a quick cardiopulmonary exam.

If myocardial ischemia is suspected:

1. Place the patient on *2 L O₂* via a nasal canula, give *nitroglycerin 0.4 mg SL Q 5 min × 3* if the pain continues. If the pain is not relieved, you can give *morphine 2 mg IVP;* repeat as needed until the pain is relieved; observe systolic blood pressure (SBP) and keep it higher than 90 mmHg.
2. Place *nitroglycerin paste 1–2 inches Q6h as long as SBP is above 90 mmHg.*
3. If pain continues, consider starting *NTG drip (Tridil) 50 mg in 250 mL D5W (200 μg/mL). Start it at 5 μg/min (2 mL/h), then titrate upward by 5–20 μg/min as needed using the chest pain as an indicator.* Call the ICU and your resident to ask about the possibility of transferring the patient to the ICU.
4. Give Aspirin 325 mg PO × 1.
5. Give Heparin: load with 80u/kg IV then 25,000u in 250cc DSW at 18 u/kg/h. (Make sure you quiac the patient prior to starting heparin and to check APTT in 6 hr.
6. Make sure that the patient is on a monitor and a pulse oximeter.
7. Send for STAT CPK/MB, troponin, and chemistry.

CONSTIPATION

1. Ask about the last bowel movement that the patient had. Usually, you will learn that it occurred several days ago.
2. Check for medications that can cause constipation, especially narcotics and see if it can be substituted.
3. If there is no abdominal pain or distention, the patient has simple constipation that you may treat easily. Order an *enema,* or give *lactulose or milk of magnesia, 30 cc PO Q4h until the first bowel movement.*
4. Also start *docusate sodium (Colace) 100 mg PO BID.*

DIARRHEA

Attempt to determine the cause of the diarrhea:

1. Ask the nurse whether the patient is having signs and symptoms such as hypotension, fever, tachycardia, nausea, or vomiting.
2. Ask whether the diarrhea is associated with pain that might suggest ischemic colitis, diverticulitis, or inflammatory bowel disease.
3. Review the patient's medication profile to see whether it might cause the diarrhea. In particular, be alert for use of laxatives, magnesium-containing antacids, antibiotics, digoxin, or colchicine.
4. Ask when the patient had his or her last bowel movement. Fecal impaction can cause diarrhea.
5. Make sure that the patient is not dehydrated and has normal electrolytes. If so, start IVF and supplement electrolytes as needed.
6. If the patient has a fever, consider infectious diarrhea (*Shigella* and *Salmonella*), diverticulitis, or inflammatory bowel disease.

After evaluating the possible causes of the diarrhea, you can do the following:

1. Do a rectal exam to rule out fecal impaction and send stools for guiac evaluation.
2. Send stools for culture, ova, parasites (especially in HIV patients), *Clostridium difficile* toxin, and WBC (white blood cell) stain.
3. If the patient has fever, get two blood cultures (from two different sites), UA (urine analysis) with C&S (culture and sensitivity).
4. If the patient is dehydrated, start *NS 500 mL over 1 h, then 100–150 mL/h.*
5. If the patient is on any medications that might cause the diarrhea, stop them.
6. If the patient recently took antibiotics, consider pseudomembranous colitis as the cause of diarrhea. Start

the patient on *metronidazole (Flagyl) 250 mg PO TID* or *vancomycin (Vancocin) 125 mg PO QID* for seven days. If you suspect this condition, don't start any antidiarrheal agents as they are associated with an increased risk of bowel perforation.
7. If the patient is HIV-positive, send stools for Gram stain; acid-fast stain; WBC stain; bacterial, mycobacterial, and fungal culture; ova and parasites analysis.
8. If the diarrhea is severe, you can use *attapulgite (Kaopectate) 60–90 mL PO Q6h PRN,* or *diphenoxylate hydrochloride (Lomotil) 5 mg PO TID* until the diarrhea is controlled, then *2.5 mg PO BID*. You can also use *codeine 30 mg PO Q6h PRN.*

FALLS

1. Examine the patient and look for injuries.
2. If the patient is taking anticoagulants, pay extra attention during the physical exam to any signs of bleeding (that is, ecchymosis).
3. If the patient experiences a change in the level of consciousness, do a full neurological exam and consider getting a CT scan of the head.
4. Investigate how the patient fell—that is, tripped or felt lightheaded and fainted.
5. If the patient is diabetic, get a STAT finger stick.
6. If the patient felt palpitations or lightheadedness, get an EKG to rule out any arrhythmia or cardiac ischemia.
7. If you suspect any fractures, order the necessary x-rays STAT.
8. Document the fall (with date and time) and fill out an incident report.

FEVER

1. Make sure that the temperature is accurate. Ask the nurse to repeat it.

2. Know by which route the temperature was taken. Temperature taken rectally is the most accurate. Ask for the rest of the vital signs, as they will give you an idea of how sick the patient is.

3. If the patient was cultured in the past 24 hours, you might not need to perform a culture again. Usually, the sign-out notes when there is no need to culture again if the patient's temperature spikes.

4. If the patient is already taking antibiotics and his or her temperature spikes again, you might need to add another antibiotic or change the one currently being administered to the patient.

5. Pan-culture the patient, which includes two blood cultures (from two different sites); urine analysis, culture, and sensitivity tests; and sputum Gram stain and culture.

6. Order *acetaminophen (Tylenol) 650 mg PO (or PR if unable to give PO) Q6h PRN for a temperature exceeding 100.5°.*

7. If the temperature doesn't drop after the patient takes Tylenol or if the temperature is very high, you might need to ask for a cooling blanket.

8. If the patient is stable, wait until you get the culture back before starting antibiotics.

9. Remember that tachycardia is a physiological response to fever.

10. The following hints might help you differentiate among the various causes of fever:
    - A fever 24–48 hours after surgery can be caused by atelectasis.
    - A fever 5 days after surgery may occur secondary to pneumonia.
    - A fever 10 days after surgery might be indicative of pulmonary embolism.
    - A fever after vomiting is often due to aspiration pneumonia.
    - A decubitus ulcer or a wound can be a source of fever.
    - A Foley catheter can be a source of fever.
    - Fever with bradycardia can arise with *Legionella*

pneumonia, *Mycoplasma pneumoniae* pneumonia, or ascending cholangitis.

- Fever with hypotension indicates septic shock.
- Fever with a new onset murmur might indicate infective endocarditis.
- Fever with nuchal rigidity, headache, or change in mental status may indicate meningitis or subarachnoid hemorrhage.
- An intravenous line (especially a central line) can be the source of fever; check for tenderness and redness around the entry site.

11. If the patient is neutropenic, start antibiotics. Usually *maxipime (Cefepime) 2 g IV Q12h and vancomycin (Vancocin) 1 g Q12h* are good choices.

12. If you suspect aspiration pneumonia, start antibiotics, such as *metronidazole clindamycin 600mg IV Q8 and gatifloxacin (tequin) 400 mg 1 × QD, or piperacillin tazobacram (Zosyn) 4.5 g IV Q8h* (adjust the Zosyn dose according to the renal function).

13. If you suspect meningitis, call your resident to do a lumbar puncture (LP; remember, a CT scan of the head is necessary before you do the puncture), then start *ceftriaxone (Rocephin) 2g IV Q12h.*

14. If the patient is in septic shock, give *NS (500 mL as rapidly as possible and a maintenance dose of 100–150 cc/hr).* Then, give *vancomycin 1g IV Q12° and piperacillin/tazobactam (ZoSyn) 4.5 g IV Q8h* (adjust according to the creatinine clearance).

15. Document what you did for the patient.

GASTROINTESTINAL BLEEDING

Three types of GI bleeding are possible:

- Bright red blood or coffee-ground emesis is indicative of upper GI bleeding.
- Bright red blood per rectum is suggestive of lower GI bleeding.
- Black stools (melena) are suggestive of upper GI bleeding.

1. Find how much blood the patient has lost.
2. If the patient is taking any anticoagulants, stop them.
3. Send for STAT CBC, chem 8, and PT/APTT.
4. Order type and cross match, and 2–4 units of packed RBC (red blood cells) to be placed on hold.
5. If the patient is hypotensive, start IVF. Give *NS 500–1000 cc as rapidly as possible*, and a maintenance dose of *100–150 cc/h* (but use caution with CHF patients).
6. If you suspect upper GI bleeding, start *famotidine (Pepcid) 20 mg IV Q12h or ranitidine (Zantac) 50 mg IV Q8h.*
7. If PT or APTT levels are elevated and the patient continues to bleed, consider giving *2 units of fresh frozen plasma*. If the platelet count is low, then you can give *6–10 units of platelet infusion or 1 unit of single-donor platelets.*
8. If the bleeding is controlled, you can wait until the morning to do the necessary studies (endoscopy); otherwise, call for a GI consult.
9. If the patient becomes hemodynamically unstable, call your resident, the ICU resident, and a STAT GI consult.

HEADACHE

1. Ask about the type of headache, any decrease in level of consciousness, and the onset of the headache.
2. A simple headache with no other symptoms or change in mental status can be treated with *acetaminophen (Tylenol) 650 mg PO or ibuprofen (Motrin) 400–600 mg PO.* Ask the patient what usually works and give it.
3. There are some special circumstances requiring different tactics:
   - *A headache with a fever:* Check for nuchal rigidity; do a full neurological exam. If meningitis is suspected, consider ordering a CT scan of the head and LP. Start the patient on *ceftriaxone (Rocephin) 2 g IV Q12h* after the LP.
   - *A headache with vomiting, decreased level of con-*

sciousness: Consider intracranial bleeding. Get a STAT CT scan of the head.
- *Severe headache, "the worse headache of my life":* Consider subarachnoid hemorrhage. Get a STAT CT scan of the head. If Ct is negative and you still suspect it, you need to do an LP.
- *A headache with high blood pressure (SBP > 190):* Consider malignant hypertension. Look for papilledema.
- *A throbbing headache with auras and photophobia:* Consider migraine, especially if the patient has a history of migraine. You can give *ibuprofen (Motrin) 800 mg PO* or *sumatriptan (Imitrex) 25–50 mg PO*, if not contraindicated. You can also give *meperidine (Demerol) 50–100 mg IM and Vistaril 25–50 mg IM.* If the patient has a history of migraine, he or she will usually tell you what has worked in the past. Occasionally, *prochlorperazine (Compazine) 5-10 mg IV/IM might be effective in some patients.*
- *A recent head trauma (within 6–8 weeks)*: Consider epidural or subdural hematoma.
- *A headache with a history of arthritis:* Consider arthritis of the neck to be the cause of the headache. The pain can radiate from the neck to the head. Muscle strain can also cause this type of headache. You can give *ibuprofen (Motrin) 800 mg PO Q6h* or a muscle relaxant such as *cyclobenzapine (Flexeril) 10 mg PO.*
- *Headache with temporal pain:* Consider temporal arteritis. If you suspect this condition, start *prednisone 60 mg PO QD* and send for ESR (erythrocyte sedimentation rate).

HYPERCALCEMIA

Hypercalcemia is defined as a calcium level greater than 10.5 mg/dl.

1. Occasionally, you will be called for hypercalcemia, especially when the patient becomes symptomatic. Most likely, it will be signed out to you to check during your call and then treat if the calcium level is too high.
2. Before you determine whether the patient's calcium level is high, you need to obtain an albumin measurement and correct for calcium according to this formula: *for each 1 g/dL decrease of albumin below 4, add 0.8 mg/dL calcium.*
3. Symptoms of hypercalcemia include confusion, stupor, anorexia, nausea, vomiting, constipation, polyuria, and hypertension (HTN).
4. A total calcium level greater than 13 mg/dL should be treated immediately as follows:
   - Give *NS 1–2 L over 1 hour.*
   - Give *furosemide 40–80 mg IV every 2–3 hours* (diurese 2500/day).
   - Measure the urine volume hourly and the urine Na^+ and Mg^{++} levels every 4 hours.
   - Replace urinary losses with NS, KCl, and $MgSO_4$.
   - If all else fails, you can give *disodium etidronate (Didronel) 7.5 mg/kg IV QD for 3 days.*
   - Dialysis may be indicated.

HYPERGLYCEMIA

1. Symptoms that might be seen in hyperglycemia include the following (in order of severity of hyperglycemia): thirst, polyuria, polydypsia, musty odor on the breath, Kussmaul's breathing (deep, pauseless breathing), tachycardia, anorexia, nausea, vomiting, hyporeflexia, hypotonia, delirium, and coma.
2. The goal in hyperglycemia is to prevent diabetic ketoacidosis.
3. Make sure that the patient is not receiving D5W or any tube feeds with high sugar content.
4. For known diabetics with asymptomatic mild to moderate hyperglycemia, make sure that the patient follows

a sliding scale with *regular insulin and finger stick QAC and HS:*

< 200 mg/dL	0 units
201–250 mg/dL	2 units
251–300 mg/dL	4 units
301–350 mg/dL	6 units
351–400 mg/dL	8 units
> 400 mg/dL	10 units, then call house officer
< 60 mg/dL	Call house officer

5. Make sure that the patient continues on the insulin regimen he or she was taking at home; the admitting resident often neglects to do so. This choice will minimize the use of the sliding scale in insulin administration.
6. If the sugar continues to be elevated (higher than 400) after the use of the sliding scale to prescribe insulin, you can give another 10 units of regular insulin.
7. If all else fails, call your resident and consider starting an insulin drip.

If you suspect diabetic ketoacidosis, you need to do the following:

1. Give *NS 500 mL as rapidly as possible*, then keep it running at a rate of *100 mL/h*. Make sure that the patient does not have CHF. If so, *give 250 cc of NS bolus and 50 cc/h as a maintenance dose.*
2. Give regular insulin 5 units IV (slowly) then start an infusion at a rate of *0.1 U/kg/h NS.*
3. Call your resident and the ICU resident to transfer the patient to the ICU and further management.

HYPERKALEMIA

1. True hyperkalemia is defined as serum K^+ exceeding 5.0 mEq/L.

2. Symptoms that might be seen with hyperkalemia include weakness, paresthesia, decreased deep tendon reflexes, and flaccid paralysis.
3. Make sure that the patient is not taking any K^+ supplements. If so, stop these therapies.
4. Order a *12-lead EKG*. The progressive EKG changes seen with hyperkalemia are (progressing in order of the severity of hyperkalemia) defined as follows:

peaked T waves → ST segment depression → low R waves amplitude → PR interval prolongation → small or flat P waves → wide QRS complex → sine wave pattern.

The following subsections indicate the treatment recommended for specific sets of symptoms.

Mild Hyperkalemia (K^+ < 6.5 mEq/L and No EKG Changes)

1. Correct the cause, if one can be found.
2. Give *sodium polystyrene sulfonate (Kayexalate) 30 g in 100 mL of 20% sorbitol PO Q4h* (you can also give it as *50 g in 200 mL of 20% sorbitol by retention enema for 30–60 min Q4h*).
3. Recheck the K^+ level in 2 hours.
4. If the problem is not corrected, you can repeat the Kayexalate treatment.

Moderate Hyperkalemia (K^+ = 6.5–8.0 mEq/L, with Peaked T Waves Only)

1. Correct the cause, if one can be found.
2. Get a *12-lead EKG* and place the patient on continuous EKG monitoring.
3. Give *Kayexalate 30 g in 100 mL of 20% sorbitol PO Q4h*.
4. Give *D50W 50 mL IVP*, followed by *regular insulin 5-10 units IV*.

Severe Hyperkalemia (K$^+$ > 8.0 mEq/L, with Advanced EKG Changes)

1. Call your resident.
2. Correct the cause, if one can be found.
3. Get a *12-lead EKG* and place the patient on continuous EKG monitoring.
4. Give *calcium gluconate 5–10 mL of 10% solution IV over 2 minutes* to protect the heart.
5. Give *Kayexalate 30 g in 100 mL of 20% sorbitol PO Q4h.*
6. Give *sodium bicarbonate 1 amp IV × 1.*
7. Give *D50W 50 mL IV* followed by *regular insulin 5–10 units IV.*
8. Give *3 ampules of NaHCO$_3$ and 20 units of regular insulin in 1000 cc D10W and run it at a rate of 75 cc/ h*
9. If all else fails, consider emergency hemodialysis.

HYPERTENSION

1. Ask whether this event represents a new onset of hypertension and not a chronic case.
2. Ask whether the patient is taking any antihypertensive medications. If so, were there any missed doses?
3. Check whether the patient is on IVF. Often, patients left on IVF experience hypertension secondary to increased intravascular volume. If so, stop the IVF.
4. Do not drop the blood pressure more than 25% during the first 2 hours.
5. A medication commonly used to control acute hypertension is *clonidine (Catapres) 0.1 mg PO × 1*. Recheck the patient's blood pressure in one hour. You can repeat this step again if the blood pressure remains high.
6. If the heart rate is acceptable (>70 bpm), you can prescribe *metoprolol (Lopressor) 5 mg IVP × 1.*
7. If the patient is on blood pressure medications that are scheduled to be given in a few hours, you can give them earlier.

The following subsections describe a few special circumstances associated with hypertension.

Preeclampsia and Eclampsia (Hypertension in Pregnant Women)

Give *magnesium sulfate 16 g in 1 L of D5W* (give a loading dose of *250 mL over 20 minutes, then the rest at 60–125 mL/h*). Order serum Mg Q4h, keeping it at 6–8 mmol/L.

For hypertension, give *labetalol (Normodyne) 20 mg IV slow injection,* then *40–80 mg IV Q 10 min PRN up to 300 mg.* For a drip, use a dose of *1–2 mg/min.* You may use *hydralazine (Apresoline) 10–50 mg IM or 10–20 mg IV;* repeat as needed. You may also prescribe *nitroprusside (Nipride) 50 mg in 250 mL D5W (200 μg/mL), starting at 0.3 μg/kg/min (approximately 6 mL/h for a 70 kg person); the maximum dose is 10 μg/kg/min.* Watch for cyanide toxicity by checking the patient's thiocyanate levels on a daily basis.

Myocardial Infarction (Hypertension in Patients with Chest Pain)

You can give *metoprolol (Lopressor) 5 mg IV × 1,* then *12.5–50 mg PO Q12h* (make sure to specify the following parameters: hold for SBP < 95 and HR < 55). Increase Lopressor dose according to these parameters.

You can also prescribe a *nitroglycerine IV drip (Tridil): 50 mg in 250 mL D5W (200 μg/mL) starting at 5 μg/min (2 mL/h) and titrating upward by 5–20 μg/min as needed, using the patient's chest pain as an indicator.*

Aortic Dissection (Hypertension in Patients with Chest Pain Radiating to the Back)

These patients need to be admitted to the CCU and receive a STAT vascular surgery consult. You can give *nitroprusside (Nipride) 50 mg in 250 mL D5W (200 μg/mL); start at a dose of 0.3 μg/kg/min (approximately 6 mL/h for a 70 kg person) and use a maximum dose of 10 μg/kg/min.* Administer this therapy with a beta blocker to keep the patient's heart rate down. You can give *propranolol (Inderal) 1 mg IV Q 2 min* until you achieve a pulse of 60 or a total dose of 0.15 mg/kg in any 4-hour period. You may also give *labetalol (Normodyne) 20 mg IV slow injection,* then *40–80 mg IV Q 10 min PRN up to 300 mg*. For a drip, use a rate of *1–2 mg/min*.

Pulmonary Edema (Hypertension in Patients with Shortness of Breath)

These patients need to be admitted to the CCU. Prescribe a *nitroglycerine IV drip (Tridil): 50 mg in 250 mL D5W (200 μg/mL), starting at 5 μg/min (2 mL/h) and titrating the dose upward by 5–20 μg/min*.

Subarachnoid Hemorrhage (Hypertension in Patients with Neck Stiffness and Headache)

Call for a STAT neurosurgery consult.

Hypertensive Encephalopathy (Hypertension in Patients with Headache, Vomiting, and Changed Mental Status)

Transfer the patient to the CCU. You can give *nitroprusside (Nipride) 50 mg in 250 mL D5W (200 mcg/mL); starting at 0.3 mcg/kg/min at a maximum rate of 10 mcg/kg/min. Watch for cyanide toxicity with high doses by checking daily levels of thiocyanate.* Another option is to give *labetalol (Normadyne) 20 mg IV slow injection,* then *40–80 mg IV Q 10 min PRN up to 300 mg. You can also start an infusion of 0.5–2 mg/min*.

Rebound Hypertension

When antihypertensive medications (beta blockers, central-acting alpha blockers, or ACE inhibitors) are stopped abruptly, a patient may develop rebound hypertension. You need to restart the medication again, then taper the dose down slowly.

Cocaine-Induced Hypertension

Give *propranolol (Inderal) 1 mg Q 2 min IV to maximum dose of 8 mg.*

Amphetamine-Induced Hypertension

Give *chlorpromazine (Thorazine) 1 mg/kg IM.*

HYPOGLYCEMIA

1. Symptoms of hypoglycemia include diaphoresis, palpitations, tachycardia, hunger, tremulousness, confusion, anxiety, and coma. This condition can also present with focal neurological deficits.
2. Make sure that the patient is not taking excess insulin or oral hypoglycemics and is eating well.
3. Repeat the finger stick and send for chem 8.
4. If the patient is able to drink, give some juice. You should also give *50 mL of D50W IV.*
5. If there is no IV access and the patient is unable to eat, give *glucagon 0.5–1.0 mg SC or IM × 1.*
6. If the patient is NPO or is not eating, start *D5W or D10W at a rate of 100 cc/h.*

HYPOKALEMIA

1. Make sure that the patient is asymptomatic and that his or her vital signs are stable.
2. Symptoms of hypokalemia include weakness, cramps, tetany, decreased deep tendon reflexes, paresthesia, ileus, polyuria, flaccid paralysis, and cardiac arrest.
3. Look for obvious causes, such as diarrhea, use of diuretics, or use of antibiotics.
4. EKG changes associated with hypokalemia include flat T wave, PVCs, PACs, U wave, and ST segment depression.

The following subsections highlight treatments for specific types of hypokalemia.

Serum K⁺ < 3.0 mmol/L

1. Get a *12-lead EKG* and keep the patient on EKG monitoring.
2. Give *KCl 10 mEq in 100 cc NS (or D5W) over one hour × 3.* (Each 10 mEq of KCl raises the serum K⁺ by 0.1 mmol/L.)
3. Give *K-dur or KCl 20-40 mEq PO Q4 × 2.*
4. Recheck the serum K⁺ after the IV KCl is given.

Serum K⁺ = 3.1−3.5 mmol/L

1. Give *K-dur or KCl 40 mEq PO Q4 × 2.*
2. You can recheck the serum K⁺ in 4 hours or with the morning labs.

HYPOMAGNESEMIA

Hypomagnesemia is defined as a serum level of magnesium that is less than 1.8 mg/dL. The most common cause of this condition is chronic alcoholism. Other causes include malnutrition, malabsorption, diarrhea, and consumption of certain medications (loop diuretics, amphotericin B, cisplatin, aminoglycosides, and cyclosporine).

1. Because hypomagnesemia can also result in hypokalemia and hypocalcemia, it's a good idea to check serum K⁺ and Ca⁺⁺.
2. Signs and symptoms of hypomagnesemia include lethargy, confusion, nystagmus, muscle fasciculations, tremor, ataxia, and Chvostek's and Trousseau's signs.
3. Check the patient's renal function.
4. Treatment depends on the patient's magnesium level:
   - **For serum Mg⁺⁺ < 1.5 mg/dL:** Give *MgSO₄ 2 g in 100 cc D5W over one hour* and *MgOH 311 mg PO Q4 × 2.* Recheck the serum Mg⁺⁺ in 2 hours.

• **For serum Mg^{++} = 1.5–1.8 mg/dL:** Give *MgOH 311 mg PO Q4* $\times$ *3* and recheck the patient's serum Mg^{++} level in the morning.

HYPONATREMIA

1. Repeat the sodium analysis to confirm the values.
2. Symptoms of hyponatremia include confusion, lethargy, weakness, nausea, vomiting, seizure, and coma.
3. Try to look for the cause of the hyponatremia and correct it, if possible.
4. Analyze the serum and urine osmolarity and electrolyte levels.
5. Assess the patient's volume status.
6. In cases of volume depletion (involving vomiting, bleeding, dehydration, and similar problems), calculate the sodium deficit:

$$\text{Na} + \text{deficit (mEq)} = (\text{serum Na}^+ \text{ desired} - \text{serum Na}^+ \text{ observed}) \times \text{TBW}$$

where

Total body water (TBW) = 0.6 $\times$ patient's weight in kg
Excess water (L) = current TBW − normal TBW

7. Remember that 1 L of NS contains 154 mmol of Na$^+$.
8. In case of volume excess, place the patient on *1 L free-water restriction* and give *Lasix* as needed to correct the volume access (start with *40 mg IVP*).
9. When you correct the Na$^+$, do it slowly in patients with acute hyponatremia (less than 24 hours). The rate of correction should never exceed 1.5–2.0 mEq/L/h or 20 mEq/L/day.

The following subsections highlight treatments for particular types of hyponatremia.

Iso-osmolar Hyponatremia (Pseudohyponatremia)

This condition is hyponatremia with normal serum osmolality and can be caused by hyperlipidemia or hyperproteinemia. To treat it, correct the cause.

Hypovolemic Hyponatremia

Causes of hypovolemic hyponatremia include vomiting, diarrhea, pancreatitis, peritonitis, and diuretics.

1. If the patient is taking diuretics, discontinue them.
2. Replace the lost Na^+ and fluid with NS. Replace one-third of the lost sodium deficit over six hours and the rest over 24–48 hours.

Euvolemic Hyponatremia

Euvolemic hyponatremia is caused by SIADH (syndrome of inappropriate antidiuretic hormone).

1. To treat this condition, correct the cause (most commonly CNS trauma and infections, small cell carcinoma of the lungs and pneumonia).
2. Implement a free-water restriction to 1000 cc/day.
3. Diurese with Lasix.
4. Check the patient's electrolytes every 4 hours.
5. Prescribe *demeclocycline 300–600 mg PO BID*.

Hypervolemic Hyponatremia

Hypervolemic hyponatremia may be caused by CHF, nephrotic syndrome, or cirrhosis with ascites. To treat it, place the patient on fluid and salt restriction.

Hyperosmolar Hyponatremia

May be due to infusion of glucose, mannitol, or glycine leading to the shift of the intracellular fluid to the extracellular fluid resulting in decreased serum sodium. For each

100 mg/dL serum glucose above 100 mg/dL, sodium drops by 1.6 mEq/L.

HYPOPHOSPHATEMIA

1. Symptoms may develop when the patient's phosphorus levels fall below 1.0 mg/dL.
2. Symptoms include hemolysis, skeletal myopathy, and metabolic encephalopathy.
3. To treat hypophosphatemia, prescribe the following therapies:
   - Neutro-Phos 1 capsule or packet PO QID.
   - Or, K-Phos 1–2 tab PO TID/QID.
   - For severe hypophosphatemia (less than 1 mg/dL): K-Phos 0.08–0.16 mmol/kg IV over 6 hours.

HYPOTENSION

1. Check the rest of the vital signs and determine whether the patient is symptomatic.
2. If the patient is symptomatic, place him or her in the reverse Trendelenburg position.
3. Start the patient on IVF *(500 mL NS as rapidly as possible).* If the blood pressure does not improve, you can administer another 500 mL of NS. (Use caution in patients with CHF, however.)
4. Place the patient on oxygen (2 L N/C).
5. If the patient does not respond to IVF, call your resident; consider using pressers and transfer the patient to the ICU.

Following are some hints that might help in determining the cause of the hypotension:

- If the patient is on antihypertensives, hold them. These medications might cause the drop in blood pressure.
- If chest pain is present, consider MI (cardiogenic shock)

or cardiac arrhythmia. Get an EKG and treat the patient as if he or she were having an MI.

- If the hypotension occurs a few hours after the administration of IV contrast agents or antibiotics, consider anaphylactic reaction as a diagnosis.
- If fever is present, consider septic shock as a diagnosis.
- If the patient is taking anticoagulation therapy, consider bleeding to be the cause.
- If the patient is bradycardiac, consider vasovagal attack, autonomic dysfunction, or heart block as possible causes.

INSOMNIA

1. *Temazepam (Restoril) 15 mg PO QHS PRN* is a good choice for elderly patients.
2. In sedated patients, *diphenhydramine (Benadryl) 25 mg PO × 1* is a good choice.
3. If you have the time, talk to the patient and obtain a sleeping habit history. The patient might also be depressed, which could cause him or her to develop insomnia.

NAUSEA

1. Look for the etiology of the nausea, such as medication, ulcer, or another medical condition.
2. After investigating the cause of nausea, you can prescribe any of the following medications:
   - *Prochlorperazine (Compazine) 5–10 mg PO or IM Q6h PRN.*
   - *Promethazine (Phenergan) 12.5–25 mg PO/IM/PR Q6h PRN.*
   - *Trimethobenzamide (Tigan) 200 mg IM/PR Q6h PRN.*
   - For patients on chemotherapy: *granisetron (Kytril) 10 μg/kg IV over 5 minutes, 30 minutes prior to chemotherapy, or 1 mg PO BID for 1 day only.* You can

also give *ondansetron (Zofran) 32 mg IV over 15 minutes, 30 minutes prior to chemotherapy.*

OLIGURIA

Oliguria is defined as a urine output of less than 400 mL/day or less than 20 mL/h.

1. Check the latest lab tests to ensure that the BUN/Cr (blood urea nitrogen/creatinine) levels are normal and that the patient is not experiencing kidney failure. If recent lab results are not available, order new ones.
2. Determine whether the oliguria cause is prerenal, renal, or postrenal (obstructive):
   - *Prerenal:* Give IVF, *NS at 100 cc/h.*
   - *Postrenal:* If the patient already has a Foley catheter emplaced, ask the nurse to flush it with 20–30 mL of NS to ensure patency. If the patient does not have a Foley catheter at present, emplace one. If the initial urine volume on catheterization exceeds 400 mL, the patient will experience immediate relief. If all else fails, order renal ultrasound tests in the morning.
   - *Renal:* Search for the renal cause and make sure that the electrolyte levels are normal, especially the potassium level. Review all medications taken and make sure that none is causing the failure. If the cause is renal, give *furosemide (Lasix) 40 mg IV over 2–3 minutes.* If the patient does not respond to this administration of Lasix, double the dose and administer it every hour; go from 40 mg to 80 mg to 160 mg in three hours for a total of 400 mg (if you give more than 100 mg, don't infuse the drug at a rate greater than 4 mg/min to avoid autotoxicity). You can also give *metolazone (Zaroxolyn) 5–10 mg PO* to enhance the potency of Lasix (it should be given a half hour prior to Lasix). If Lasix fails, give *bumetanide (Bumex) 0.5–1.0 mg IV.* If all else fails, the patient might require urgent dialysis.

PRONOUNCING DEATH

Four criteria need to be fulfilled to pronounce someone dead:

- The patient does not respond to verbal or painful stimuli. The painful stimulus can be induced by pressing on the sternum or on the fingernail beds.
- The patient does not have any heart sounds or a carotid pulse.
- The patient does not have spontaneous respirations or evidence of air entry in the lungs.
- The pupils are dilated and fixed.

1. Document all findings in the chart, including the time you pronounced the patient dead.
2. Inform your resident and attending physician.
3. Unless the attending physician or resident instructs you otherwise, call the family and inform them of the death. Ask them if they would like an autopsy to be done. One way to tell the family of the death is to say the following: "This is Dr. X. I am calling you in regard to Mr. Y (the patient's name). I am sorry to inform you that Mr. Y has passed away." (Try not to use the word "expired.") Ask the family if they would like to see the deceased now. If they do, you can hold the body on the floor until they arrive. Most families will expect the death of the patient and your call.
4. Before your call ends, go to the admitting department and sign the death certificate.

SEIZURE

1. Ask about the type of seizure experienced by the patient and determine whether he or she is still seizing.
2. Ask whether the patient has a history of seizures or is taking seizure medication. If the patient has a history of seizures and has been prescribed seizure medica-

tions, check his or her latest levels. If no recent levels are available, order STAT ones.

3. Make sure that there is no obvious cause of seizure, such as trauma (a fall), medication, hypoglycemia, electrolyte abnormalities, infection, or acid–base imbalance.

4. Ensure that the patient is lying in the lateral decubitus position to prevent the tongue from falling posteriorly, blocking the airway, and to minimize aspiration.

5. Get a finger stick and correct it accordingly.

6. Send for chemistry, CBC with differential, calcium, magnesium, and albumin; also order pulse oximetry, followed by a STAT ABG if it is abnormal.

7. Use the following treatment regimen:
   - Treat the patient only if the seizure lasts for more than three minutes.
   - Give *diazepam (Valium) 2 mg/min IVP* until the seizure stops or you reach a maximum dose of *20 mg*. You can also give *lorazepam (Ativan) 2–4 mg IV over 3–5 minutes*.
   - Load the patient with *fosphenytoin 15–20 mg/kg IV (usually you can give 1000–1500 mg) IV at a rate no faster than 100–150 mg/min*.
   - Give *thiamine 100 mg IV over 3–5 minutes* and *D50W 50 mL IV*. If the patient is hypoglycemic, the seizure should then stop.
   - If the seizure persists, call for a neurology consult, STAT EEG, CCU resident, and your resident. The patient might be in status epilepticus and might require admission to the ICU.

SHORTNESS OF BREATH

1. Order pulse oximetry immediately; if it is low, order an ABG.

2. Get more details about the SOB: How long has the patient had it? Did it start suddenly or gradually? Is the patient in distress? Is the patient experiencing other

symptoms, such as chest pain, palpitations, nausea, vomiting, or lightheadedness?

3. Does the patient have a history of lung disease, such as chronic obstructive pulmonary disease (COPD), asthma, pulmonary embolism (PE).

4. Place the patient on O_2, keeping the pulse oximetry higher than 93%. If the patient has a history of COPD and is a CO_2 retainer, keep the O_2 level as low as possible (1–2 L N/C).

5. Examine the patient and listen to his or her lungs, checking for wheezing, rales, and crackles to differentiate between possible causes of SOB.

6. Order a STAT portable chest X ray.

7. Make sure that the patient has IV access.

The following specific circumstances might help differentiate the etiology of SOB.

Central Depression

1. The respiratory rate is less than 12.
2. Possible etiologies include use of narcotics, use of sedatives, stroke, and intracranial hemorrhage.

Pain and Anxiety

1. The respiratory rate is greater than 20.
2. The patient is anxious or in severe pain.
3. Treat the pain.
4. Calm the patient down.
5. Consider prescribing *lorazepam (Ativan) 1–2 mg IV × 1.*
6. If the patient has a history of anxiety, prescribe *alprazolam (Xanax) 0.25 mg PO Q8h PRN.*

Pneumonia

1. The patient might be febrile.
2. Pneumonia may be associated with cough, fever, sputum production, and unilateral or bilateral crackles.

3. The pneumonia might be preceded by aspiration.
4. Send for a chest X ray and sputum Gram stain and culture.
5. The following treatments are recommended for specific groups of patients:
   - **Outpatient (community-acquired) pneumonia:** Give *cephtriaxon (Rocephin) 1 g IV Q24h and azithromycin (Zithromax) 500 mg IV × 1 dose, then 250 mg PO QD × 4 days.*
   - **COPD:** Give *ampicillin 1 g IV Q6h.*
   - **Aspiration pneumonia:** Give *piperacillin/tazobactam 4.5g IV Q8° (adjust dose according to renal function).*
   - **Elderly patients:** Give *cefuroxime (Ceftin) 750 mg IV Q8h.*
   - **Alcoholics:** Give *cefazolin (Ancef) 1–2 g IV Q8h and gentamicin 1.5–2 mg/kg IV loading dose, then 1–1.5 mg/kg IV Q8h.*

Pulmonary Embolism

1. The patient might present with tachypnea.
2. The SOB has a sudden onset, is sometimes associated with unilateral crackles, and pleural friction rub might also be present.
3. Look for DVT or risks of PE.
4. EKG changes are noted on the following parameters: S_1, Q_3 (S1 wave in lead I, Q wave in lead III), right axis deviation, and RBBB (right bundle branch block).
5. The ABG shows respiratory alkalosis, PO_2 of less than 80 mm Hg on room air, and elevated A-a O_2 gradient (equal to $(713 \times FIO_2) - PaO_2 - PCO_2/0.8$)
6. Get a STAT V/Q (ventilation/perfusion) scan. If the V/Q scan gives indeterminate results and you still suspect PE, then you can proceed with a spiral CT of the lungs or pulmonary angiogram to confirm the diagnosis. (By this time, you should have informed your resident or attending physician of the patient's condition.)
7. Start heparin as in MI (bolus and drip).
8. Monitor the patient's APTT, keeping it 1.8–2.8 times more than the normal values.

Congestive Heart Failure

1. The patient usually has a history of cardiac disease.
2. Associated symptoms include orthopnea, PND (postnasal drip), elevated JVD (jugular venous distention), and the presence of S_3 and bibasilar rales.
3. Give *furosemide (Lasix) 40 mg IV over 2–3 minutes* and monitor the patient's urine output and symptoms. If he or she does not improve, double the dose to *80–160 mg IV Q1h for a maximum dose of 400 mg* (for doses exceeding 100 mg, the infusion rate should not exceed 4 mg/min). You can also give *metolazone (Zaroxolyn) 5–10 mg PO* to enhance the potency of Lasix (it should be given a half hour prior to Lasix).
4. If Lasix does not work, prescribe *bumetanide (Bumex) 0.5–1.0 mg IV.*

Asthma

1. The patient will wheeze throughout the lungs on auscultation.
2. Patients usually report a history of asthma.
3. Place the patient on O_2 N/C or a face mask, keeping the O_2 saturation level above 93%.
4. Give *albuterol 0.5 mL in 3 mL NS and ipratropium (Atrovent) 0.5 mL in 3 mL NS nebulizer Q4–6h;* the first dose should be given STAT.
5. Prescribe *methylprednisone (Solu-Medrol) 60 mg IV Q6h.*
6. If you identify any signs of infections, start the patient on antibiotics. You can give *ceftriaxone (Rocephin) 1 g IV Q24h* and/or *azithromycin (Zithromax) 500 mg IV × 1 dose,* then *250 mg IV QD × 4 days.*

COPD Exacerbation

1. On auscultation, you hear crackles and wheezes throughout the lung and poor air entry.
2. The patient typically reports a history of COPD and/or smoking.

3. Follow the same treatment outlined for asthma.

Myocardial Infarction

1. Other symptoms associated with MI include chest pain radiating to the left arm, diaphoresis, lightheadedness, nausea, vomiting, and/or numbness of the left arm.
2. You might see EKG changes.
3. Refer to the "Chest Pain" section for management recommendations.

Respiratory Failure

1. This condition is diagnosed when PO_2 is less than 60 mm Hg or PCO_2 exceeds 50 mm Hg, with a pH of less than 7.30 on room air.
2. Look for the cause and correct it.
3. Call your resident and the ICU resident for possible intubation.

TRANSFUSION REACTION

1. Common signs and symptoms include fever, chills, chest pain, SOB, diaphoresis, back pain, hypotension, tachypnea, urticaria, and pulmonary edema.
2. Stop the transfusion immediately.

The following management strategies are recommended for specific types of transfusion reactions.

Anaphylaxis

1. Give *epinephrine 0.2–0.5 mL of 1:1000 solution SC*. You may repeat this therapy every 15 minutes, if needed.
2. Administer *NS 1000 mL bolus.*
3. Give *diphenhydramine (Benadryl) 50 mg IV × 1.*
4. Give *hydrocortisone 250 mg IV × 1.*
5. Intubation might be indicated.

Acute Hemolytic Reaction

1. Administer *NS 500 mL bolus.*
2. Maintain urine output at 100 mL/h.
3. Give *furosemide (Lasix) 40 mg IV × 1.*
4. Send blood for the following analyses: cross and match, Coombs' test, free HB, CBC, PT, PTT, BUN, creatinine, and electrolytes.

Urticaria

1. You may continue the transfusion.
2. Give *diphenhydramine (Benadryl) 50 mg PO or IV × 1.*
3. Give *acetaminophen (Tylenol) 650 mg PO × 1,* if fever is present.

Pulmonary Edema

1. Patient usually presents with an acute onset of SOB and appears to be very ill.
2. Other associated signs and symptoms include tachypnea, diaphoresis, S3, elevated JVD, bilateral crackles, and frothy and blood-tinged sputum.
3. Place the patient on 100% O_2 face mask.
4. Keep the patient in an upright, seated position.
5. Order a STAT ABG and chest x-ray, CPK/MB, troponin, electrolytes, and an echocardiogram to evaluate the left ventricular function.
6. Give *furosemide (Lasix) 40 mg IV over 2–3 minutes and monitor the patient's urine output.* If the patient does not respond to this administration of Lasix, double the dose and administer it every hour; go from 40 mg to 80 mg to 160 mg in three hours for a total of 400 mg (if you give more than 100 mg, don't infuse the drug at a rate greater than 4 mg/min to avoid autotoxicity). You can also give *metolazone (Zaroxolyn) 5–10 mg PO* to enhance the potency of Lasix (it should be given a half hour prior to Lasix). If Lasix fails, give *bumetanide (Bumex) 0.5–1.0 mg IV.* You can also consider Lasix drip *(500 mg/50 cc undiluted, starting at 10 mg/h and titrating it upward according to I/O).*

115

7. Give *morphine 2–5 mg IVP.*
8. Give *Nitroglycerin tablets 0.4 mg SL.* Then, start *Tridol drip (50 mg in 250 cc D5W starting at 5 mcg/min and titrating upward using blood pressure as a parameter).*
9. Intubation might be indicated.
10. Your resident and the ICU resident should be involved in the patient management at this point.

VOMITING

Refer to the "Abdominal Pain" and "Nausea" sections for management recommendations.

The following types of emesis are possible:

- *Frank blood*: indicative of upper GI bleeding.
- *Vomiting food after fasting:* indicative of gastric stasis or gastric outlet obstruction.
- *Coffee-ground:* suggestive of upper GI bleeding.
- *Vomiting with acute onset of pain:* can signify perforated viscus, peritoneal irritation, or acute pancreatitis.
- *Pain relieved with vomiting:* suggestive of bowel obstruction.
- *Vomiting several hours after the onset of pain:* suggestive of intestinal obstruction or an ileus.

REFERENCES

1. Ahya SN, Flood K and Paranjothi S. The Washington manual of medical therapeutics, 30th ed. Philadelphia: Lippincott Williams & Wilkins, 2001.
2. Braunwald E, Fauci AS, Kasper DL, Hauser SL, Longo DL and Jameson JL. Harrison's principles of internal medicine, 15th ed. New York: McGraw-Hill, 2001.
3. Fishman MC, Hofman AR, Klausner RD and Thaler MS. Medicine, 4th ed. Philadelphia: Lippincott-Raven, 1996.
4. Marshall SA, Rudy J. On call principles and protocols, 2nd ed. Philadelphia: W. B. Saunders, 1993.
5. Tisher CC and Wilcox CS. Nephrology, 3rd ed. Baltimore: Williams and Wilkins, 1995.

6

Final Words

Your internship can be a terrifying and exhausting experience as you, the fledgling doctor, are thrust into a seemingly hostile environment. It can also be one of the single most rewarding times of your life. This book is intended to serve as a guide, by helping you minimize the negative aspects of this period so that the entire experience can fulfill its intended function—making you the best physician possible. Of course, you cannot accomplish this goal by simply reading the book; you must go into the internship program with the requisite knowledge, attitude, and health. This guide acts more as a primer for your mental and personal preparedness, to be used as a resource while you learn to interact with that vast entity called humanity.

Read this book as frequently as possible, as it will introduce the general concepts of caregiving. While the particular circumstances described in the book may differ from your actual situation, the experiences encountered will not. The Boy Scout motto, "Be Prepared," is as true for interns today as it was for boys decades ago. Recognize that your medical knowledge will carry you only so far as an intern; along the way, you must blend a variety of organizational, management, and personal skills together with this knowledge.

In addition to taking into account your individuality and unique perceptions, remember the results of the surveys (Chapter 2). Your concept of a "good intern" may differ radically from the views held by other members of your team. As a consequence, you may have to alter your conceptions a bit. You can certainly remain true to your own style and beliefs, but you just might have to adjust them a bit as you strive to strike the appropriate balance.

One simple idea is often sadly forgotten as we become involved with our own demons: Put the patient first, last, and always. That's it—why you became a doctor, why you sacrificed so much, and why you worked so hard. If you learn nothing else from this book, remember to treat your patients with compassion and dignity.

The time from your birth to this moment has been your "becoming." The "becoming" process ends only when you die (or perhaps not). You are, above all, a student who is still "becoming" a doctor—no, not just "a doctor," but the "best doctor" possible. Use your student status aggressively and take advantage of every opportunity to learn from those around you. To limit your tutors to only physicians would be a mistake; absorb knowledge from anyone who will take the time to teach you. Not only will you learn something that may save a life, but you will also increase another person's self-esteem at no expense to your own ego. Some strange souls hoard their knowledge in a miserly fashion, parceling out bits and pieces grudgingly, if at all. Don't follow this course. Remember the patient? By passing on your expertise to someone else, you positively influence the care given to the patient. Your knowledge and intelligence are gifts—not rights—so share them with others.

Will your internship be difficult? Yes, it will, . . . but you will prevail. Become comfortable with this book and its concepts, because what you learn during your internship will remain with you throughout your career. You have certain talents that have enabled you to study medicine and become a doctor. While some artists work with words or clay, your medium will be the blood and sinew of a life. There is no finer endeavor. Good luck.

Index